Thomas Starr King, Orville Dewey

The New Discussion of the Trinity

Containing notices of Professor Huntington's recent defence of that doctrine

Thomas Starr King, Orville Dewey

The New Discussion of the Trinity
Containing notices of Professor Huntington's recent defence of that doctrine

ISBN/EAN: 9783743407688

Manufactured in Europe, USA, Canada, Australia, Japa

Cover: Foto ©ninafisch / pixelio.de

Manufactured and distributed by brebook publishing software (www.brebook.com)

Thomas Starr King, Orville Dewey

The New Discussion of the Trinity

THE

NEW DISCUSSION OF THE TRINITY;

CONTAINING NOTICES OF

PROFESSOR HUNTINGTON'S

RECENT DEFENCE OF THAT DOCTRINE,

REPRINTED FROM "THE CHRISTIAN EXAMINER," "THE MONTHLY RELIGIOUS MAGAZINE," "THE MONTHLY JOURNAL OF THE UNITARIAN ASSOCIATION," AND "THE CHRISTIAN REGISTER."

TOGETHER WITH

SERMONS,

BY REV. THOS. STARR KING, AND
DR. ORVILLE DEWEY.

BOSTON:
AMERICAN UNITARIAN ASSOCIATION.
1867.

INTRODUCTORY NOTICE.

The following articles are mostly reprinted from various periodicals. The Sermon by Dr. Dewey, which closes the volume, has not been published before, and the Discourses by Mr. King are reprinted from a pamphlet.

The occasion of all these papers was a sermon of Dr. Huntington, in which, after having occupied a Unitarian pulpit for a long number of years, he asserted and defended the Church doctrine of the Trinity. Such an event made it necessary for his brethren and friends in the Unitarian ranks to reconsider their position. When one so able and earnest as Dr. Huntington was led to renounce the doctrine they had so long preached in common, a due respect to him, as well as regard to the truth, required them to give a careful and patient attention to his reasons.

The results of the re-examination of their doctrinal position appeared in several articles in Unitarian periodicals, and sermons from Unitarian pulpits. The arguments of Professor Huntington were in general candidly examined and fully answered. The result of the discussion is apparently not unfavorable to the Unitarian side of the question. None of the reasons of Professor Huntington seemed weighty enough to change the views of his former friends, or to induce any of them to imitate his example. When the dust of the conflict cleared away, the forces of the Unitarians were found occupying their former position, or perhaps one a little in advance.

The result would perhaps have been different if Professor Huntington had reached any new and large statement of the Trinity, which should take up into itself and harmonize the old antagonisms. Such a statement might have carried the whole Church forward to a higher and more commanding platform. But when, instead, he only fell back on the old formulas, he confessed his inability to reconcile the contradictions which had so long separated persons equally intelligent, pious, and sincere. The old Trinitarian statement had never satisfied Unitarians, — the Unitarian statement had not satisfied Trinitarians. Obviously, therefore, a new statement was needed, more comprehensive and profound than either. Merely to reassert the old doctrine, was to leave the difficulty where he found it. To declare that the majority of the Church was on the side of the Trinitarians, was to utter a truism. To contend that the Trinity was the only source of Christian piety and humanity, was to hazard a generalization somewhat larger than the facts seemed to warrant. Consequently, the new position taken by Dr. Huntington is significant only as regards himself, insignificant as regards the general doctrinal tendencies of the Church. Its only meaning is that the Trinity suits his peculiar tendency of mind better than the Unity.

CONTENTS.

	Page
DR. HUNTINGTON ON THE TRINITY. From the Christian Examiner	1
PROF. HUNTINGTON'S ARGUMENT FOR THE TRINITY. From the Monthly Journal of the A. U. A.	45
TRINITARIANISM NOT THE DOCTRINE OF THE NEW TESTAMENT. By REV. T. S. KING	90
DR. HUNTINGTON ON THE TRINITY. By REV. E. H. SEARS	144

COMMUNICATIONS TO THE CHRISTIAN REGISTER: —

I. DR. HUNTINGTON'S MISQUOTATION OF NEANDER ON THE TRINITY. By E. A.	161
II. DR. HUNTINGTON'S QUOTATIONS FROM SCRIPTURE IN PROOF OF THE TRINITY. By E. A.	169
III. DR. HUNTINGTON AND DR. POND. By R. P. S.	176
IV. LETTER FROM PROF. HUNTINGTON	181
V. REVIEW OF DR. HUNTINGTON'S LETTER. By E. A.	189

VI. Gradual Development of the Doctrine of the Trinity. By E. A. 197
VII. The Doctrine of the Trinity in the Fourth Century. By E. A. . . . 209
VIII. Further Illustrations of Neander's Views, and of Dr. Huntington's Quotations, with a Practical Improvement of the Subject. By E. A. 217

The Primitive Christian Creed. By Rev. Orville Dewey, D. D. 225

DR. HUNTINGTON ON THE TRINITY.*

[From the Christian Examiner.]

Christian Believing and Living. Sermons by F. D. HUNTINGTON, D. D., Preacher to the University, and Plummer Professor of Christian Morals in Harvard College. Boston: Crosby, Nichols, & Co. 1860.

IN the volume of Sermons thus designated we gratefully acknowledge a rich contribution to homiletic literature, and not only so, but a real addition to the sentimental life of the time. Dr. Huntington gives proof in these discourses of a special vocation for the preacher's office, not always or often manifest in otherwise able and worthy divines. A born *ecclesiastes*, and not merely a man of fine powers, who from taste or accidental determination has assumed the function. It needs something more than distinguished ability, — more than learning and "humane eloquence," however coupled with purity of manners and acquiescence in the creed of the Church,

---

* The extra-large edition of the Christian Examiner for March, 1860, in which this article appeared, having been exhausted, the proprietor of that journal permits its republication in this volume.

— to fully furnish the preacher of the Gospel. It needs, above all other graces and gifts, a religious nature and an ecclesiastical spirit. And these Dr. Huntington exhibits in an eminent degree. He possesses that quality, half intellectual, half moral, — that combination of the spiritual mind and the earnest soul, fervid temper, and devout imagination, — which constitutes what may be termed a genius for religion. As a preacher to the conscience and the feelings on topics of spiritual life and purely practical import, he has few superiors in this generation. No candid reader, however he may criticise and repudiate the author's theological views, can fail to perceive or refuse to acknowledge the evidences of strong religious sensibility and spiritual fervor which broadly pervade and distinguish these compositions.

But the more decided his gift and success in his own legitimate province, the more we regret that he should ever turn aside from the inculcation of practical truth to argue questions of speculative theology, where at once his want of the necessary qualifications for such discussion, and the discrepance of abounding zeal and defective knowledge, of dazzling assurance and dim apprehension, are painfully apparent. There are few to whom it is given, like the great preachers of reviving Christendom in the twelfth and thirteenth centuries, to unite intellectual vision, dialectic subtilty, and spiritual depth with the popular gift of practical discourse. Dr. Huntington is not one of these. He discourses much better than he sees, and is abler in illustrating given truths than he is in discriminating truth from falsehood. The moment he enters the domain of theology proper, we miss the scientific mind which religion needs not, but which theology may not dispense with. We miss the intuitive as well as the dialectic faculty. We miss the penetration and critical tact, and, more than all, the learning, which are needed to light up effectually the dark questions of divinity, or to make the discussion of them profitable, or even — to thoughtful minds — tolerable.

The Sermon entitled "Life, Salvation, and Comfort for Man in the Divine Trinity," the most elaborate in this collection, illustrates our remark, provoking criticism not so much of the views maintained as of most of the reasoning employed in their defence. Coming from one whose former position was known to be adverse to the doctrine here professed, whose sermon of five years since, to that effect, is still fresh in the minds of many, and who therefore stands before the public in the attitude of a recent convertite, this particular sermon has awakened an interest by no means due to its real value as compared with the rest of the volume. Its interest is that of confession, not of thought. Our first impression of it raised in us the question: For whom was it written? For the learned or the unlearned, laymen or theologians? It seemed to us equally unfitted for either class. Dr. Huntington surely could not suppose that his exposition of the doctrine he discusses, and his reasoning about it, would be satisfactory to theologians of any school. He must have felt the inadequacy of his statement and defence to meet the requirements of Biblical scholars. And yet, on the other hand, considered as addressed to a mixed audience, the sermon, notwithstanding its fervid tone and fascinating unction, is in the dogmatic and expository parts of it too abstruse and metaphysical for popular edification. As a theological argument, competent critics will regard it as worthless. Dr. Huntington does not seem to us to have even understood the real import of the dogma he so zealously maintains, still less its historic origin and doctrinal bearings.

It is not necessary to a full and conscientious reception of any doctrine, that one should be able to defend it with logical or theological proofs. A man's confession may be sincere, although his apprehension be imperfect and his reasons inadequate. We believe in the Augustinian maxim which puts faith in religion before understanding. *Fides præcedit intellectum.* But when the confessor of a doctrine does undertake to expound and to teach it, — when, moreover that confessor is also Professor in a learned University, — and when especially, as in this case, he has come to his adopted views from another confession and creed, — we expect the *intellectus* also. And this is precisely what we miss in this discourse. In our comments upon it we wish it understood once for all that we are not arguing against the Trinity* as conceived by the early Church, and expressed in the so-called Apostles' Creed; our polemic relates solely to

---

* We use this word, in deference to ecclesiastical custom, to denote the aboriginal Christian doctrine of Father, Son, and Holy Ghost, — i. e. of a God self-revealing in his Word and self-communicating by his Spirit. The word Trinity (*trinitas*, τριάς), which, late in the second century or early in the third, was used to express this idea, by emphasizing the numerical element, unintentionally colored it with something alien. The universal prevalence of the doctrine itself in the early Church is patent to every

Dr. Huntington's view, which confounds that doctrine with an ecclesiastical and metaphysical Tripersonality, and proposes a philosophem of after ages as a fundamental article of the Christian revelation. A triad of Christian sanctities — Father, Son, and Holy Ghost — is one thing; the doctrine of Tripersonality, whether true or false, is another and a very different thing. The last is no part of the Gospel, so far as the Gospel is expressed in the writings of the New Testament. Nor is it the creed of the early Church. Dr. Huntington confounds the two in one assertion, and concludes them both in one evangelical authority. It is this tripersonality of God, as expressed in the pseudo-Athanasian Creed, which he affirms to be the true evangelical Trinity, — the doctrine of the New Testament. When this notion is thrust dogmatically forward as one of the essentials of the Christian faith, as of binding authority, and as Scripture doctrine, we feel it to be a falsity and an offence. And knowing as we do that many well-meaning and pious Christians cannot find in it the "Life, Salvation, and Comfort" which Dr. Huntington promises, but, on the contrary, are much disturbed when that is urged as divinely authorized

---

student of ecclesiastical history. It appears conspicuous in various monuments which have come down to us, — among others, in the clumsy figure of Ignatius (Epistle to the Ephesians), which represents Christ as the pulley and the Holy Spirit as the rope by which we are hoisted to God.

It is matter of regret that the "Unitarians" of a former generation were led by their needful and timely protest against Trinitarian dogmatism into a position of seeming hostility, and, in some cases, of real indifference, to this doctrine.

Gospel truth, with which their own consciousness cannot adjust itself, we feel bound to protest against the assertions and assumptions of this plea.

It is somewhat unexpected to find ourselves in the year of grace 1860 gravely reiterating what Trinitarian scholars of critical repute now concede, that the dogma of the Tripersonality is not the doctrine of the New Testament. Nor can we be expected to retrace in detail the weary commonplaces of this debate. We have neither the spirit nor the space to lug forth and spread out the mouldy straw which other generations have threshed so soundly. All the arguments which human wit could devise to extort from the Scripture a confession of the Three Persons, have been disposed of before Dr. Huntington came upon the stage. The books which contain them and the answers to them have long been gathered to their kindred dust in the "dumb forgetfulness" of old libraries. Let those who are curious seek them there. We shall not resuscitate them. Our purpose is confined to a brief examination of some of Dr. Huntington's positions.

With obvious reason, the preacher has chosen for the text of his discourse the solitary passage of the New Testament in which "Father," "Son," and "Holy Ghost" are named together (Matt. xxviii. 19), and from which the Church in after time derived the baptismal formula. He finds in these words "a ministry, an initiatory ordinance, a creed." And the creed, according to him, is "the Triune name." Here at the threshold a wanton misstatement and a gross perversion of the fact. Three names are mentioned, Father,

Son, and Holy Ghost. Of triunity, of the three-in-one or the one-in-three, not a syllable, not the faintest intimation. The words were uttered at the parting of Jesus with his disciples. "Now if ever," says Dr. Huntington, "Christ will distinctly proclaim the doctrine of Christendom." Be it so! If then the doctrine of Christendom, according to the intent of the Master, were the Tripersonality of God, "Christ will distinctly proclaim" it. Has he done so? He has proclaimed three sanctities. Of triunity, of tripersonality, we repeat, not a word, not the faintest intimation. The attempt to find it here but proves, in the preacher's own language, "how desperate are the shifts of a determined theory." We thank him for these words, — they express precisely what we have felt at many points of his argument.

The discourse proceeds. "Our faith is summoned to the three persons of the one God: the Father, the Son, and the Holy Ghost. No hint is given that there is any difference of nature, dignity, duration, power, or glory between them. There is nothing in the situation, the relations, or the contents of the Divine formula* to suggest that either of the three is less than the others,

---

* We do not understand that our Saviour meant to prescribe in those words, "Baptizing them in the name," &c., a formula to be used in the rite of baptism, nor does it appear that the words were so construed or this formula adopted in the Apostolic age. The word ὄνομα here is redundant (see Schleusner, sub voc.), and the sentence may be rendered: "Baptizing (i. e. initiating) them into (the knowledge of) the Father, the Son, and the Holy Ghost." The Father the Supreme God, the Son the Redeemer of the world, the Holy Ghost the Sanctifier.

or less than God." Why should there be? what need of any hint? Does it necessarily follow, in the absence of any hint to the contrary, that where three are named together, the three are equal? Was it likely that those whom our Saviour addressed on this occasion would, without a "hint," infer that equality in the three here named? On the contrary, so foreign was the notion of such an equality from all Judaistic habits of thought and belief, that, had the Master intended to teach it, we must suppose he would "distinctly proclaim" it, that there might be no mistake. We therefore turn the tables, and say, No hint is given that there is any equality of nature, dignity, duration, power, or glory between them. There is nothing in the situation, the relations, or the contents of the Divine formula, to suggest that either of the three is level with the others, or that more than one of them is to be regarded as God.

"Each of them," continues Dr. Huntington, "is elsewhere in the Scriptures referred to as God. Each of them is distinguished [?] from the others by the personal pronouns. To each of them Divine attributes and Divine acts are ascribed, and to each Divine worship is offered." Waiving or granting the question as it regards the Son, where, we ask, is the Holy Ghost referred to in the Scriptures as personal God distinct from the Father? Where in the Scriptures is supreme worship offered to the Son and the Holy Ghost? "The term *Trinity* is not applied to the doctrine in the Bible, but it is a definite and just description of what the Bible teaches." If so, we agree that "there is no reason why it should not be adopted and used." Only let us see to it what we mean by Trinity, and not confound it with Tripersonality, — the baptismal confession with the ecclesiastical philosophem.

Farther on (p. 369) we read, as an argument for the personal Godhead (distinct from the other two) of the Holy Spirit: "The baptismal formula of the text would alone put the personality of the Holy Spirit on a ground of reasonable certainty through the most natural understanding of the words. . . . . . How forced would be the suppression, — and putting what a repulsive ambiguity on this final and momentous commission of the Lord's followers for the conversion of the world, — if he first mentioned two names which, as all alike agree, are names of distinct persons, and then slipped in without notice or explanation a name which purports [?] to be just as much the name of a person as the other two, but which is only a common noun signifying an immaterial influence!" Was ever such reasoning! The phrase Holy Ghost was a term in common use among the Jews of that day. It was used to denote a particular form of Divine agency, or a special effect of that agency, or a special beatitude of humanity, as where John the Baptist says of the coming Christ: "He shall baptize you with the Holy Ghost and with fire." It was spoken of, not as a being distinct from God, with a separate life and volition, but as God himself in that particular manifestation, or God's reflection and witness in man. Why should Christ then stop to explain what none of his hearers, we have reason to suppose, would be likely to mistake? Dr. Huntington's position in regard to this passage is, that where three are named together, and two of the three are persons, it follows that, without an explanation to the contrary on the part of the speaker, the third must be understood to be a person also. We know of no grammatical or rhetorical rule which necessitates such an inference, especially where, as in the present case, the third is distinguished by the neuter pronoun from the other two, which are masculine. If it were so, the converse would be equally true, — that where two of the three are impersonal, the other must be impersonal also. And so we might infer the impersonality of the Holy Spirit from 1 John v. 8. If the "water" and the "blood" are not personal, then neither is the "spirit" personal according to this way of reasoning.

In the Supper discourse (John xiv., xv., xvi.) our Saviour, it is true, as the preacher remarks, personifies the Holy Spirit with the word παράκλητος, which our version renders Comforter. But no unprejudiced reader can fail to perceive that the personification here is purely rhetorical. "And I will ask the Father, and he shall give you another Comforter, that he may be with you forever; *the spirit of truth,* which* the world cannot receive because it seeth it* not, neither knoweth it;* but ye know it, for it stayeth by you and shall be in you. I will not send you away orphans, I am coming to you." Mark how Jesus identifies the Comforter with himself. It is his own influence which they are to experience after he is gone, and which will be to them as if he returned to them in person. And so

---

* Not *whom* and *him,* as in our version. We translate from Tischendorf's text.

in the other three passages of this discourse, in which the Holy Spirit is designated by the word Comforter. It is not spoken of as a separate existence, but as an influence proceeding from God and Christ, whose agency is personified by that term. The difference between a rhetorical personification and an apodictic declaration of personality is too obvious to need elucidation. The preacher asks: "In those tender and solemn conversations, charged with the only hope and counsel to the disciples about to be bereaved, and indeed to the world of mankind, is it possible that our Saviour was dealing in dark paradoxes or uninterpreted figures of rhetoric?" It is not only possible, but an undeniable fact, as the preacher, were he more familiar with the Scripture to which he appeals, and less inaccurate, would have known. Not to speak of the figure of the "house of many mansions," and the "way," &c., and the figure of the "Vine," which occupies with its amplifications a third part of the fifteenth chapter, our Saviour emphatically declares, toward the close of this discourse, — referring to what he had been saying, — "These things have I spoken unto you in proverbs, but the time cometh when I shall no more speak unto you in proverbs, but I shall show you plainly of the Father." The word here rendered "proverb," παροιμία, signifies that very thing against which the preacher protests, — "dark paradoxes." See Schleusner, who defines the word, in its application to this passage, "sententiam gravem, obscuram, abstrusam et per figuras propositam . . . . . sermonem obscuriorem et intellectu difficiliorem qui explanatione eget."

And now we come to a passage wherein it is impossible to acquit the author of either great carelessness of statement or great disingenuousness. "Many other passages in the Gospels and Epistles can be wrested from their obvious meaning" — that is, of the personality of the Spirit — "only by a similar violence. It is so with the Apostolical benedictions, which were evidently intended to be what they have so generally proved, the familiar repositories and oft-repeated symbols of the great central facts of Christian theology.* Apart from some preconceived purpose, who would ever suppose there was a sudden lapse or deviation from the personal to the impersonal style, on getting half or two thirds through that worshipful and preeminent blessing, 'The grace of our Lord Jesus Christ and the love of God and the fellowship of the Holy Ghost be with us all evermore'?" Now what is the obvious understanding of this passage, and the allegation contained in it? The writer is speaking of the personality of the Holy Spirit; it is doing violence, he maintains, to the language of his text not to find it there, as also in the fourteenth and fifteenth chapters of John; and then, in the passage we have cited, he pleads that this is the obvious meaning of *many other passages* in the Gospels and Epistles, which can only be wrested from that meaning by "similar violence." He does not specify one of those passages by so much as a reference to chapter and verse, but, hiding himself in a prudent vagueness, he continues, "It is so with the Apostolical benedictions." The Apostolical benedictions, then, he would have it inferred, (from his use

---

* A dangerous admission, this, for a "Trinitarian."

of the plural,) as a general rule, make mention of the Holy Spirit, and that in the sense of a person. But what is the fact? In the twenty-one Epistles and the Apocalypse there occur — including the opening with the closing — some forty benedictions. Out of these forty, more or less, there is *only one in which the Holy Spirit is so much as mentioned.* In all the rest, it is either Christ alone that is referred to, as, "The grace of our Lord Jesus Christ be with you;" or God with Christ, as, "Grace unto you, and peace, from God our Father and the Lord Jesus Christ." We can hardly conceive of a stronger proof of the truth of our position, that the modern Trinitarian doctrine is not the doctrine of the New Testament, than precisely this fact. If the Apostles had had the Trinity in their minds, how could they have so ignored it? If Dr. Huntington was not aware of this fact, he was not qualified to discuss this subject. If he *was* aware of it, and still used the vague plural, then "how desperate are the shifts of a determined theory"!

One case, however, there is, out of all these benedictions, in which the Holy Ghost is joined to the names of God and Christ. It is that referred to by Dr. Huntington, of 2 Cor. xiii. 14, "The grace of the Lord Jesus Christ, and the love of God, and the communion* of the Holy Ghost, with you all!" On this the preacher thus comments: "Apart from some preconceived purpose, who would ever suppose there was a sudden lapse or deviation from the personal to the impersonal style, on getting half or two thirds through that worshipful and

---

* ‘Η κοινωνία, communication, or participation in common.

pre-eminent blessing?" To which we reply, that without some preconceived purpose, no one surely would dream of maintaining, that because Jesus Christ whose favor, and God whose love, the Apostle invokes for his Corinthians, are persons, therefore the Holy Spirit, which he prays may be communicated to them, is personal also. "When," says Neander, "a man intrenches himself in some particular dogmatic interest, and makes that his central position, he can easily explain everything in conformity with his own views, and find everywhere a reflection of *himself.*" For our own part, so different is the look of this passage to us, so decided its leaning in the opposite direction, that, if we were searching for Scriptural arguments against the distinct personality of the Holy Spirit, as separate from that of God and of Christ, this would be one of our proof-texts. Three names are named. To the first two, personal attributes — favor and love — are ascribed. The third is distinguished from the other two, in that no such attributes are connected with it, but that, on the contrary, it is spoken of as something diffusive and extended, — a quality, an influence, not a person in any legitimate sense of the word.

Strange as it may seem, considering the length of this sermon, which occupies more than sixty pages of a closely printed, middle-sized volume, we have already exhausted the author's Scriptural argument in defence of the Tripersonality. The Deity of Christ is a separate question; we speak of that portion of the argument only which bears directly on the doctrine of the Trinity. Divested of the prodigal trail of nebulous matter which accompanies it, the solid argument — the comet's nucleus — amounts to this: that when Jesus ordained his disciples to baptize the nations into the Father, the Son, and the Holy Ghost, he meant to assert (since he did not deny) the co-equality of these three, consequently, the tripersonality of the Godhead; — further, that the Father and the Son being persons, it follows that the Holy Ghost must be personal also, and a person distinct from the other two; — and lastly, that Christ personifies the operation of the Holy Spirit in John xiv., xv., and xvi. This is all; this is the proof that Tripersonality is the doctrine of the New Testament.

Perhaps we ought not to quarrel with the inadequacy of the reasoning, were it only candid. Dr. Huntington has made the most of his material: the fault is in the problem, not in him. The problem of proving that doctrine from the Bible is a desperate one, suggesting "desperate shifts" in those who undertake its solution. These shifts are nothing new. The interpolation of 1 John v. 7 — a memorable circumstance in this connection — proves plainly enough what the old theology sought in the Bible and failed to find there. The interpolation is a signal confession of that failure, a standing witness to the fact that the doctrine of Tripersonality is not the doctrine of the Bible. By no desperate shifts, by no ecclesiastical cross-questioning, by no exegetical torture, can the Bible be made to confess the dogma of the Athanasian God. It is not in the Old Testament, it is not in the New. Those who receive it do so on other authority than that of the sacred canon. Whatever the Church may have been in time past, whatever it may be in this present, it is certain that the Bible is not — in the sense we are discussing

— Trinitarian. For those with whom the Bible is, in matters of theology, the supreme court of last appeal, a candid examination of the Scripture will settle the question of the binding authority as an article of faith, if not of the abstract truth, of the doctrine.

A word or two further on some points of this discourse.

Dr. Huntington insists, with reiterated emphasis, on the fact of the wide, and, as he supposes, almost universal reception of this doctrine. We do not deny, that, taking into view the entire period of the Christian Church, a great majority of Christians have been nominal receivers of the "Trinitarian" creed; that is, have belonged to churches in which the Tripersonality was an article of faith, and have seemingly acquiesced in the symbol. How many of this vast multitude have thought sufficiently about it to be called believers in any proper sense, and, of those few who have really exercised their minds upon it, how many have heartily embraced it, we can never know. The preacher pleases himself with a fancy sketch of worshipping assemblies the Christian world over, who, with whatsoever differences of circumstance and place, shall unite in ascriptions of praise to the Father, the Son, and the Holy Ghost,— ascriptions, by the way, in which most Unitarians would heartily join. And hence he would have us infer that all these believe in the Tripersonality; for he adds as it were a definition of the Three, "the one ever-living and almighty God of all the earth." We fancy that scarcely one in the thousand of all these worshippers ever troubles his brain with the dogma of Tripersonality. They who do so most likely dismiss it presently, as something which the doctors must settle for themselves, but which they for their part can make nothing of. If this be claimed as faith in the Athanasian Trinity, we cheerfully concede whatever of corroboration the ecclesiastical dogma may draw from that fact. "It is this truth," says the preacher, "which has kept its vigils by the weary processions of sufferers, and consoled them." We cannot of course disprove the truth of this assertion regarding a matter of which Omniscience alone can know. But we vainly attempt to figure to ourselves the husband bereft of the wife of his youth, the mother at the grave of her first-born, the orphaned child, turning for support and consolation, not to the blessed declarations of Him who proclaimed himself the "Resurrection and the Life," — "In my Father's house are many mansions," not to the lofty strain of St. Paul, "For we know that if our earthly tabernacle-house were dissolved," &c.; but — for this is the Trinity which Dr. Huntington advocates — to the comfortable words of the "Athanasian" Creed: "Whoever will be saved, before all things it is necessary that he hold the Catholic faith. Which faith except every one do keep whole and undefiled, without doubt he shall perish everlastingly. And the Catholic faith is, that we worship one God in Trinity and Trinity in Unity, neither confounding the Persons nor dividing the Substance," &c., — propositions which, whether they be true or false, would seem but imperfectly suited to such straits. The same consolations are not available for all. For one Christian mourner who is comforted by the thought of the Trinity, there are thousands and hundreds of thousands who seek consolation in prayers to the Virgin, and do abundantly find it. But Mariolatry, though not without its æsthetic charm, would poorly comfort us whose "consolation aboundeth by Christ."

We are not insensible to the argument from numbers. Theoretically, we allow it some considerable weight as a general rule of presumptive evidence. But practically, in any given case, we have to modify it by other considerations. Had we lived in the fifteenth century, and been of a critical, inquiring mind, we should probably have had this problem presented to us, — whether to receive or reject the Church doctrine of Transubstantiation. We should have found the argument from numbers and authority almost irresistible. The doctrine clearly prefigured in the Fathers. From the eighth century on, the leading authorities all on that side. And had we then had access to the Scriptures we should there have found — what? No doubtful text, but explicit declarations of our Lord, necessitating, if the doctrine were denied, what might seem to be desperate shifts of figurative interpretation in order to escape the binding conclusion of the sacramental *metabole*. And yet we should then most likely, as now, have found in our own consciousness a countervailing force which would not have suffered us to be of the Catholic Church in that particular.

We respect Catholicity, but when it is urged as a ground of belief, we recall what was said by a Catalonian bishop of the eighth century in answer to Alcuin, who attempted to refute him by appealing to the general consent of the Church. "I believe in a Catholic Church," said Felix, "founded by Christ and diffused through the world, but the Church is sometimes vested in a few individuals." *Aliquando vero ecclesia in exiguis est.*

But what is the extent of Catholicity which after all can be fairly claimed for the doctrine in question? Dr. Huntington, confounding ecclesiastical determinations which date from the latter part of the fourth century with the simple baptismal confession of preceding ages, speaks as if the doctrine of three co-equal persons in the Godhead had been from the first the creed of Christendom.* His language is, "a tenet so emphatically and gladly received in *all the ages* and regions of Christendom as almost literally to meet the terms of the test of Vincentius, — ' Believed always, everywhere, and by all.' " Suppose we strike out from the term of ages comprised in this assertion three centuries, or three and a half, to begin with. The truth of history demands this discount, if we speak of a common belief in the co-equality of Father, Son, and Holy Ghost. If the general reception of the "Athanasian" Creed be the test, some centuries more must be added to the three. But waiving that, and taking for our limit the authori-

---

* If Dr. Huntington means to be understood as placing the confession of belief in Father, Son, and Holy Ghost, which, though not demonstrably of Apostolic institution, is doubtless very ancient, in the same category with the doctrine of a three-person God, and as applying the assertion of belief in the Trinity to that confession, we shall not differ with him regarding the antiquity and universality of the Trinitarian doctrine. But neither, in that case, can we understand the aim of his advocacy. If he allows the name of Trinitarian to all who believe in Father, Son, and Spirit, against whom is he contending? Whom does that definition exclude?

zation * of the doctrine of Consubstantiality as applied both to Son and Spirit, we have the year 380 † as the true date of the institution of the Trinitarian faith, which then became the established and self-styled "Catholic," although by no means the universal, creed of Christendom. The Council of Nicæa, which half a century earlier affirmed the consubstantiality of the Son, had left undetermined the nature of the Spirit; and Gregory Nazianzen, on the very eve of the final settlement, says: "Some of our theologians consider the Holy Spirit to be a certain mode of the Divine agency, others a creature of God, others God himself. Others say they do not know which of the two opinions they ought to adopt out of reverence for the Holy Scriptures, which have not clearly explained this point." Hilary of Poicters, one of the foremost men of that century, and second to none in spiritual authority, though leaning strongly to Homoousian views, "held it best to remain fast by the simple Scripture doctrine concerning the Holy Spirit, which, as it seemed to him, furnished no materials for exact logi-

---

* The authorization was long anterior to the general reception, if, indeed, we can speak of general reception at all in this connection.

† Date of the Theodosian edict, followed, in 381, by the Council of Constantinople, where the ecclesiastical sanction was added to the imperial. The character and conduct of this Council would be sufficient of themselves to cast suspicion on the doctrine it affirmed. Gregory Nazianzen, himself a Trinitarian, condemns and repudiates it. It passes for one of the universal Councils, but has no more title to that designation than any local and *ex parte* synod.

cal definitions of this doctrine." "Should one ask us," he says, "what is the Holy Spirit, and we knew of nothing further to reply than that he exists by and from Him by whom and from whom are all things, — that he is the spirit of God, but also God's gift to believers, — and this answer displeased him, then might the Apostles and Prophets also displease him; for they also affirm only this of him [the Spirit], that he exists." *

Until the accession of Theodosius, "the first of the Emperors baptized in the true faith of the Trinity," A. D. 380, it was, humanly speaking, an "even chance" whether Christendom would be Trinitarian or Evangelical in its pneumatology. Nay, even the Christology, even the consubstantiality of the Son, affirmed by the Council of Nicæa, was still debated with incalculable issue. For fifty years the tongue of the balance wagged uncertain; now this scale dipped, now that. The imperial soldier threw his sword into the Homoousian, and — the Catholic Church was born.

"It is our pleasure that all the nations which are governed by our clemency and moderation should steadfastly adhere to the religion which was taught by St. Peter [!] to the Romans...... According to the discipline of the Apostles and the doctrine of the Gospel, let us believe the sole Deity of the Father, the Son, and the Holy Ghost, under an equal majesty and a pious Trinity. We authorize the followers of this doctrine to assume the title of *Catholic* Christians; and as we judge that all others are extravagant madmen, we brand them with the impious name of Heretics; and declare that their conventicles shall no longer usurp the

---

* Quoted from Neander.

respectable appellation of churches. Besides the condemnation of Divine justice, they must expect to suffer the severe penalties which our authority, guided by heavenly wisdom, shall think proper to inflict upon them."

The penalties followed in the course of a few weeks. A military inquisition was established, the clergy who refused to accept the creed thus ordained were expelled from their churches, and a fine, equivalent to two thousand dollars, was imposed on every one who should "dare to confer, or receive, or promote an heretical ordination."

Christians are wont to charge the Moslem with having established his religion by force. If ever religion in this world was established by force, it was the Trinitarian faith. The Roman *fiat* was the judge that ended the strife where Greek wit and reason failed. Providentially, as we can see, for the education of the human race for whom it furnished, if not "a guide to everlasting life," a substantial mystery for the exercise of awe and wonder, through the "gloomy vale" of the Middle Age. Providentially, but not therefore decisive of the absolute truth.

Gibbon seems to insinuate that the action or decision of Theodosius was the product of external and accidental motives. "Once indeed he expressed a faint inclination to converse with the eloquent and learned Eunomius, who lived in retirement at a small distance from Constantinople. But the dangerous interview was prevented by the prayers of the Empress Flaccilla, who trembled for the salvation of her husband; and the mind of Theodosius was confirmed by an argument adapted to the rudest capacity." The argument was the well-known trick of the Bishop of Iconium. The Emperor and his son were seated on a throne. The wily ecclesiastic bowed with profound obeisance to the father, but treated the young prince with the easy familiarity of an equal. The Emperor ordered his arrest for this insult, and received the premeditated answer: "Thus, O Emperor, will the King of heaven punish those who pretend to honor the Father, and refuse to honor equally the Divine Son."

It was far toward the close of the fourth century, then, that the dogma of three co-equal persons in the Godhead became the established creed of Christendom. Near four centuries, and those the first four,— a grave deduction from the "everywhere and always" of the preacher's assertion! Graver than at first it might seem. The numerical amount of the testimony of those ages is no true measure of their testimonial importance. And when we say this, we are willing to abandon the fourth century altogether, as being an era of forced conclusions on both sides. Theology was vitiated from the moment the secular power assumed its control. It had ceased to develop itself freely, and the visible Church was no longer a true witness of the faith. We make no account of Arianism in our judgment of this matter. Arianism was not beautiful, and the Arians did many unhandsome things. But certainly the Triunitarian theology had far less reason to boast of its final success than Arianism of its temporary triumphs. The character of the councils that fashioned it, in the fourth and fifth centuries, was mostly such as to justify the strong language of Scaliger: "Eorum concilia fuerunt meræ conspirationes,"—"Their councils were mere conspiracies." Socrates, a Trinitarian, pronounced that of Nicæa "a fight in the dark." Gregory, another, had probably that of Constantinople in his mind when he said of synods, "There is contention, there is strife, there the latent wickedness of cruel men is collected together." The first Council at Ephesus was a mixed mob of "Orthodox" ecclesiastics and sailors, bent on violence, and headed by the infamous and furious Cyril. The second at Ephesus, where the "fathers" were compelled by military force to sign blank papers, and where the Bishop of Alexandria beat and killed the Bishop of Constantinople, is known to history as the "Robbers' Council."* Really, when in the retrospect of history we assist at the rearing of the sin-polluted structure of the Trinitarian Catholic faith, concerning which a contemporary Trinitarian (Gregory again) complained that "the kingdom of heaven was converted by discord into the image of chaos, of a nocturnal tempest, of hell itself,"—and which caused a contemporary pagan historian to say that "the enmity of Christians toward each other surpassed the fury of savage beasts against man,"—we not only conceive a hearty disgust to ecclesiastical Trinitarianism, but find even more to respect in the prominent Paganism than

---

* For the honor of humanity it ought to be stated that the acts of this Council were annulled, and its authority disallowed, by that of Chalcedon, 451. The latter is an honorable exception to the general statement above,—a true Œcumenical Council. The dicision of that Council respecting the nature of Christ is still the highest authority in the Christian Church on that subject, the true "Orthodox" doctrine concerning Christ.

in most of the prominent Christianity of that age; and so far from wondering that the Emperor Julian abandoned the faith in which he was educated, our wonder is rather that his example was not more extensively followed. So far as we can judge at this distance of time, the balance of the virtues was not on the Christian side. Baron Bunsen, who is no Unitarian, — who justly condemns the Unitarianism of the eighteenth century as "modern Deism asking Christ for a model," — after stating "for the honor of truth" that the Trinitarian decision was a "logical contradiction," thus characterizes the ecclesiastical formation of that doctrine: "The Church history of the fourth, fifth, and sixth centuries resolves itself into two tragedies. In the fourth century one party among the clergy appeared to negative the problem, and the other solved it illogically and unhistorically. The latter view having triumphed by a persecuting and often unscrupulous majority, the victorious hierarchical party canonized, in the course of the two next blood-stained centuries, the confession of its intellectual bankruptcy into a confession of faith, and made submission to it the condition of churchmanship and the badge of eternal salvation."

Taking, then, the first three centuries only, which are not Trinitarian in the sense of this discourse, as witnesses of the truth of Christianity on this subject, we say that the authority of that testimony far exceeds its numerical amount. Those centuries outweigh in importance all the centuries that followed to the time of the Reformation, — perhaps we may add, all the centuries since. Not merely because they were chronologically nearer to the source of truth, but because in them theology developed itself freely without interference of the secular power, and without the bias of ecclesiastical prestige. When once the Catholic Church was established, and became supreme authority in matters of faith, there was forthwith an end to all independent judgment, and to all free inquiry on points already decided by that Church. Weak men were deterred by personal fear, and good men were prevented by scruples of conscience, from questioning her decisions. The theologians of the Middle Age, wise and profound and holy as many of them were, are not independent witnesses on this point.* We cannot admit their testimony as to the previous question, but only as to the *rationale* of the "mystery." They received the doctrines which the Church delivered, and interpreted them and rationalized them as well as they could within the limits of the Church confession. And some of them — indeed all the foremost of them, Anselm, Abelard, Hugo à St. Victoire, Alexander Hales, Albertus Magnus, Raymond Lull, Thomas Aquinas — explained the Trinity in such a way — they distilled and refined it to such a degree — as to leave very little that modern Orthodoxy would be willing to accept as satisfactory statement. They retained the letter indeed, but the hard, dogmatic element of it was disengaged in their alembic, and instead thereof a something was evolved, a philosophic residuum was deposited, as harmless as it was specious, and as unevangelical as it was profound, — a fancy Trinity which

---

* Neither, for the same reason, was St. Augustine, the last writer of importance on this subject before the fall of the Western Empire.

none would dispute and few would understand, and in which still fewer would recognize the Scriptural Father, Son, and Holy Ghost. In this they followed the lead of St. Augustine, their great predecessor, who in his treatise *De Trinitate,* after threading his labyrinthine way through fourteen books of exquisite subtilties in search of a proposition which shall satisfy reason, and justify dogma, and reconcile philosophy, which he loved so well, with religion which he loved more, arrives, in the fifteenth, at this conclusion, that the Divine Trinity consists in Wisdom, Self-consciousness, and Self-love.* Infinite Wisdom is the Father, his Self-consciousness the Son, his Self-love the Holy Spirit. God, the absolute Being in the act of self-consciousness becomes two, — Being and Knowing. In the love with which he perpetually seeks himself — i. e. wills the good — he becomes three. But this love is also the union of the first and second; in it the three are one. Thanks to the glorious Father for suggesting a transcendental solution, which, though it does not touch the evangelical right of the dogma, reveals in it or imports into it a philosophic idea.

In the swelling catalogue which Dr. Huntington recites, of names addicted to the Trinitarian creed,† we find but one writer prior to the fifth century. And he is the only real authority in this matter, of those here named, because the only independent witness. That writer is Athanasius, the "pillar and ground" of the doctrine. A great and venerable name! We regard

---

* "Trinitas sapientia scilicet, et notitia sui et dilectio sui."
† See foot-note to page 361.

the man with immense admiration. So far as the authority of an individual can avail in such matters, that of Athanasius must be allowed. Still it is but a fallible individual that testifies, with no better means of knowing than ourselves. The rest of Dr Huntington's vouchers are representatives of foregone conclusions, heirs to a dogma not to be questioned, but defended and explained, — most of them Churchmen sacramented to the service of ecclesiastical establishments based on the Tripersonality. Some of them never thoroughly investigated it; others, like Bishop Taylor, rather tolerated than embraced it. We press this imposing cloud of witnesses, and it yields but one drop, after all, of valid testimony, — the single Athanasius. Names more to the purpose might have been found. One secular philosopher, like Leibnitz or Lessing, who might both have been cited in this connection, would outweigh, in point of independent testimony, the whole brood of ecclesiastics. Protestantism, it is true, like Romanism, has been mostly "Trinitarian." The schism was not a dogmatic one;* the Church split on right and discipline, not on questions of theology; and where ordinance and polity were not concerned, the old authority still pressed. But Protestantism, since the sixteenth century, has been growing continually less Trinitarian, and exhibits already a powerful array of genius and learning opposed to the Athanasian faith.†

---

* "It must strike every one as strange," says Baur, in his History of the Doctrine of the Trinity, "that, in the period beginning with the Reformation, the dogma of the Trinity was made so little the subject of independent theological investigation." — *Einleitung*, p. 106.

† A faith which lacks the testimony of Milton, Newton, Locke,

We have thus exposed the fallacy of Dr. Huntington's appeal to numbers, by showing that, for want of the important and decisive testimony of the first three centuries, the rest is vitiated and essentially neutralized. The first three centuries were not Trinitarian in the sense of this discourse. We do not mean to assert that no form or kind of Trinitarianism appears in them. In the Alexandrian school, through the influence and with partial adoption of Pagan, that is of Platonic ideas, there developed itself in opposition to, or parallel with, the Monarchianism which prevailed in the West, a species of Trinity, which, so far, however, from answering to the modern Trinitarian dogma of the co-equality of three persons in the Godhead, is known as the system of "Subordination," maintaining as it did, with rigorous discrimination, the inferiority of the Son to the Father, and that of the Spirit to the Son. Origen, the chief representative of this "Subordination System" in the East, proves

---

to say nothing of the hosts of minor and later celebrities which might be named, will do wisely to say little of its allies this side of the Reformation, and had better confine its appeal to ante-Protestant times. Dr. Huntington affirms that "the ascendant school of philosophical thought to-day is unequivocally Trinitarian." The grave audacity of this statement is too comical for serious discussion. In any other connection we could view it only as a piece of pleasantry. A certain Pope was anxious to carry a point in his Council of State. The ballot was thrown, the vote was decidedly adverse. "Gentlemen," said his Holiness, "it is very desirable that the vote for this project should be unanimous," — and, taking his skull-cap from his head, and covering with it the negatives, "It is unanimous."

Trinitarian indeed! We wish we could say it was even Christian.

the subjection of the Son to the Father, and his dependence on the Father, from the idea of God as the one absolute principle. "So surely as the only uncreated First Cause is above all that he has made, — the principle of Truth above the truth, the principle of Light above the Light, the Original above the image, — so surely the Son can be conceived only as inferior to the Father."* "The all-connecting God and Father acts upon each individual thing, imparting to each, as absolute Being, out of his own, their individual being. Less than the Father is the Son, whose action extends only to rational beings; still less than the Son is the Holy Spirit, whose action is confined to the saints."†

The subordination of the Son to the Father, and the Spirit to the Son, is expressed with equal distinctness by Tertullian, who, together with Cyprian and Novatian, represented this system in the West. Tertullian, early in the third century, was the first who made use in this connection of the word *Trinitas*, translating and enlarging the Greek Τριάς. "The Church," he says, "is properly and principally that Holy Spirit itself, in which is a *trinity* of one divinity." ‡ And this perhaps is the nearest approach in the way of phraseology to the later Triunitarian idea, although the word Divinity has not precisely the import here which our modern associations connect with it. Tertullian does not mean to say that the Church is level with God, but that, by

---

* Baur, *Lehre von der Dreieinigkeit*, &c., Vol. I. p. 197.

† Ibid.

‡ "Nam et ecclesia proprie et principaliter ipse est Spiritus, in quo est trinitas unius divinitatis." Hagenbach, *Lehrbuch der Dogmengeschichte*, Dritte Auflage, pp. 98, 99.

the Holy Spirit which is in it, it is made, together with Christ, partaker of the Divine nature. It appears, however, that even this imperfect development of the Trinitarian doctrine encountered then, as the finished dogma has since, the charge of tritheism, and that the majority of Christians opposed it on that ground. We find Tertullian complaining that the greater portion of believers in his day were afraid of this economical triplicity (*expavescunt ad œconomiam*). "They say that we preach two and three Gods, while they worship only one." * This Subordination theory formed the transition from the Unitarianism † of the first and second centuries to the fully developed Trinitarianism of the fourth.

If Dr. Huntington's Scriptural argument is, as we

---

* We must, therefore, demur to such statements as that of Neander, that the economical and practical doctrine of the Trinity constituted from the first the fundamental consciousness of the Catholic Church," as likely to mislead, though not demonstrably false. The belief in one God, the Father, in the Son, and in the Holy Ghost, was the general confession of the Church, so far as we know, in the first century. And this is all that can be affirmed. There was no idea of Trinity here; the fact of the threeness was no part of the " Catholic consciousness ;"— and when the attempt was made to define this confession, to emphasize the numerical element in it, and to shape it into a speculative system, the "Catholic consciousness" resisted the movement. Neander, with other historians of the Church, confounds sometimes the Catholic consciousness with the opinions of prominent individuals.

† Of which there were two kinds, Humanitarianism, represented by the Ebionites, and afterward by the Artemonites, and the belief in the supreme deity of Christ, whose confessors were known by the name of Patripassians.

have shown, preposterously inadequate, and his plea of popularity a fallacy, what shall we say of his metaphysical speculations and attempted philosophic illustrations of his theme? We can see in them only an unconscious confession of "intellectual bankruptcy," and a melancholy proof of mistaken vocation. We have room but for one or two examples in this kind.

In a style sufficiently imposing, and reminding one of some Gnostic theogony, he thus propounds his fundamental theses: "In the transcendent, removed, and awful depth of his Absolute Infinitude, which no understanding can pierce, the Everlasting and Almighty God lives in an existence of which our only possible knowledge is gained by lights thrown back from revelation." Pausing here for a moment, we ask, Is not this one everlasting and true God of whom the preacher speaks the same with him whom our Lord named Father, and whom we are taught to call our Father in Heaven? This we had supposed to be the common belief of Christians, but Dr. Huntington preaches another Gospel. "Out of that ineffable and veiled Godhead,—the groundwork, if we may say so, of all Divine manifestation or theophany,—there emerge to us in revelation the three whom we rightly call persons, Father, Son, and Holy Ghost, with their several individual offices, mutual relations, operations towards men, and perfect unity together." The Father then is not the Everlasting and Almighty God, but a second term, an impersonation, a proceeding from God. Father, Son, and Spirit are persons; the Almighty God is not a person, but an impersonal "groundwork," from which the Father emerges, just as the Hindoo trinity has a Being behind it, — the Brahma, a Brahm. In effect, we have here, instead of a Trinity, a Quaternity; — 1. the Almighty God; 2. the Father; 3. the Son; 4. the Holy Ghost. But, the preacher may say, the three last-named constitute together the first. Then why not put it so? According to the language we have cited, it is the one that makes three, instead of the three making one. Why talk of the "groundwork" at all, especially since he immediately adds, "We know of no priority to that Threeness, of no Deity independent of that threefold distinction." Observe the contradiction; he first speaks of the Almighty God as existing behind the "Threeness," — the groundwork thereof, — and then declares, that we know of no such Being; he speaks of "an existence of which our only possible knowledge is gained by lights thrown back from revelation," and then denies that any such existence is revealed, or is even conceivable. "We conceive of God always, not as Absolute Being, but as in relations, in process, in act. And in such relations, process, act, we behold him only as Three." In short, Dr. Huntington distinguishes between the Father and the absolute God, and, in vindication of this distinction, obscurely suggests* that "human language could not so well represent these infinite realities as by using the same term 'Father' sometimes [!] for the absolute Godhead and sometimes for that relative paternal Person in the Godhead brought to view only when the Son and the Spirit appear." Unless we have read the New Testament our life long in vain, the term "Father" is *always* used

---

* Page 371, near the bottom.

for the absolute Godhead, and no other "Father" and no other Godhead is recognized or intimated from Matthew to Revelation. St. Paul says, "To us there is but one God, the Father, of whom are all things, and we in him; and one Lord Jesus Christ, by whom are all things, and we by him." "Howbeit," he continues, — one could almost fancy, with prophetic allusion to the Plummer Professor, — "there is not in every man that knowledge." We do not say that this distinction between God and the Father is altogether new; but we do say, that this is not the Catholic and Orthodox idea of the Trinity. According to that idea, the "Father" is identical with the absolute Godhead, is simply a name for that Godhead. The Son is generated from the Father, the Holy Ghost proceeds from the Father and the Son; but the Father at least is ultimate and absolute. This is the idea of the New Testament, and the one which especially pervades every page of the Gospel of John.

A curious instance of the author's confusion of mind, and want of logical as well as critical discrimination, occurs on page 367, where he rashly undertakes to comment on the daring and sublime prophecy of Paul to the Corinthians, (1 Cor. xv. 24 – 28,) in which the Apostle predicts the final cessation of the Mediator's office and the Son's divine reign; — the passage of all others in the New Testament least favorable to Dr. Huntington's views, but which he endeavors to pervert to his own use by "private interpretation," and bungles deplorably in so doing. "At last, when all the purposes of the propitiation are accomplished, — in that dim, far-off, well-nigh inconceivable future, ... this incarnate 'Head over all things to the Church' will render up the kingdom to the Father and *resume* his place in the co-equal Three, the indivisible One." Resume his place! So then at present, and until that "far-off, well-nigh inconceivable future," the Son has no place in the co-equal Three. Who occupies it meanwhile? Or is the second Person in abeyance? Commentators have inferred from this passage a final cessation of the Trinity; Dr. Huntington would seem to infer a postponement of it until the end. We should really like to know, for curiosity's sake, what the author had in his mind when he penned these words; we confess our own "intellectual bankruptcy" here. Paul declares, in the most unmistakable terms, that a time will come when Christ, having put all things under his feet, shall no longer reign, but shall "himself be subject unto Him that put all things under him, that God may be all in all." Dr. Huntington calls this a resuming of his place in the "co-equal Three;" that is, he shall continue to reign, and not "be subject." As Macaulay said of one of Basil Montagu's proofs of the innocence of Lord Bacon, "We know no way of answering such arguments except by stating them."* We are reminded, by this attempt to make white black, of the work of one Meyer, written to prove the doctrine of the Trinity from the Old Testament alone.† The text on which he principally relies as being, on the whole, "the most clear and conclusive," is Deut. vi. 4, "Hear, O Israel, the Lord our God is one Lord."

"It would seem to require some audacity" to handle Paul in such a fashion, yet not, perhaps, more than was

---

* We quote from memory, and are not sure of the precise words.

† De Mysterio S. S. Trinitatis ex solius Veteris Testamenti Libris demonstrato.

needed to enunciate the following sentence, in which the author browbeats simple folk for using words in the only sense in which they are capable of being understood: "What shall be said of the mental proportions of men who persist in the dull fallacy of imputing to believers in the Trinity of God, who is a Spirit, the notion of an arithmetic relation?"* &c. Does Dr. Huntington imagine that, by mere dint of sovereign scorn, he can empty words of their obvious and only possible meaning? If Trinity or Threeness, a noun of number, does not express an arithmetic relation, what in the name of reason and of language does it express? and why make use of the term? Justin Martyr, who used to be regarded as authority in these matters, and whose "mental proportions" would perhaps compare not unfavorably with those of the author of this discourse, expressly declares that the Father and the Word are not merely logically, but arithmetically, distinct, not γνώμῃ, but ἀριθμῷ.

The word "Person" too, it seems, does not mean person in this connection,† but something quite different from what is usually understood by that term. One is driven to ask, Why write a long sermon on a subject in relation to which the principal terms em-

---

* And yet, with the strangest self-contradiction, the author subjoins in a note to this very passage (p. 379), that it will be made to appear "that it is three, not less and not more, which, in the nature of *numbers* and of forms, admits the greatest *relative* combination of simplicity and variety, and especially meets the abstract conditions of the ontological problem." Our venerated teacher in theology, when one of the youths of the class discoursed in this style, would inquire, with a dubious shake of the head: "Are you *quite* sure, Mr. ———, that you know what you are talking about?"

† See note to p. 375.

ployed are professedly discharged of their ordinary import, and become words of unknown signification?

The fact is, the metaphysic of the doctrine was always a delicate and sore point with its advocates. Although, in its present form, a genuine product of rationalism, — a pure creation of the understanding, — yet the moment the understanding offers to approach it, however reverently, with however sincere a desire to appropriate its import, it is warned off the ground as incompetent or dangerous. Candid inquirers, who would fain know what they believe, are treated with dissolving views, as children tease one another with the partial showing of some treasure not suffered to be fairly seen. The doctrine is presented as an article of faith; and when we attempt to lay hold of it with honest apprehension, it is snatched away or turned about in such a manner as to baffle scrutiny. We begin to consider the numerical aspect, and immediately it is withdrawn; we examine the Persons, and they disappear; if we would rest in the One, the Three is thrust forward; if we would analyze the Three, the One is returned upon us. "It is a mystery," we are told. "You are to believe in it, but must not look it in the face." When Roscellinus, writing in the interest and defence of the Trinity, endeavored to explain it with his "one Substance and three Things," the explanation was condemned as heresy and tritheism, and the author compelled to flee his country. The precise line of demarcation between a modality and a person — the line which separates Sabellianism from Tritheism — has never been defined; and every statement of it verges to the one or the other of these extremes. The coyness of theology on this subject derives some excuse from the fact that all attempts to seize the details of it lead to absurdities. Its ablest expounders have been guilty of such. Even Anselm, one of the wisest of theologians and of men, is betrayed into shocking platitudes and the grossest anthropomorphism. In attempting to show * why the Son rather than any other person of the Godhead should have become man, he argues that, if one of the others had assumed this condition, there would have been two sons in the Godhead, the son of Mary and the Son of God. And again, "If the Father had become man, there would have been two *grandsons* in the Trinity; the Father would have been the grandson of the parents of the Virgin, by his assumed humanity; and the *Word*, although in that case it would have had nothing human in it, would yet have been the grandson of the Virgin, because he would have been the son of her son." †

Singularly unfortunate is Dr. Huntington, and unhistorical, in his position that the doctrine of the Trinity is the great safeguard against pantheism on the one hand and against idolatry on the other.‡ Nothing is more notorious than the fact that the rise of idolatry in the Christian Church was contemporaneous with, or immediately subsequent to, the Trinitarian determinations of the fourth and fifth centuries. Equally notorious is it that the Trinitarian faiths, as, for instance, the Hindu, have been most pantheistic, and that, on the

---

* In the *Cur Deus Homo ?*
† German translation, (Erlangen, 1834,) p. 75.
‡ See pp. 381, 382.

other hand, the one religion in the world which has been, through all its periods and in all nations, entirely free from idolatry is strictly Unitarian, — the religion of Islam.

But we pass to a matter of graver import. We ventured to assert, in our opening remarks on this discourse, that its author did not understand the doctrinal bearings of the dogma he has undertaken to defend. With an evident desire to be orthodox in his theology, he is not orthodox according to any standard known to us, certainly not according to any standard of the Catholic Church. He attempts to join what the Church has put asunder, and professes what the Church has condemned. The proof of this assertion is found in his application of the doctrine of the Trinity to that of the Atonement.* In his exposition of the latter doctrine, he makes the idea of a *suffering* God an essential and pivotal point. Now the truth is, this idea, so far from being a constituent element in the orthodox doctrine of the Trinity, as applied to the Atonement, is even — as the preacher would have known, had he fathomed the meaning of the doctrine, or studied its historic development — incompatible with and antagonistic to it. He infers that Deity suffered together with humanity in Christ, from the nature of the union between the two. "But the union of the two natures was real, organic, — not apparent only, not dramatic, nor mechanical; so that when the Saviour suffered, God suffered." (p. 390.) Now it belongs to the very essence of the Trinitarian creed, — that is, to its doc-

---

* See pp. 386 *et seq.* to 395.

trine concerning Christ,— that the union of God and man in the person of the Redeemer was not a *fusion* of the two natures into one *nature*,* but a co-ordination and conjugation of the two in one *person*. The person is one, the natures are two. Christ is not — if we may use such language without irreverence — a cross between Deity and humanity, but perfect God and perfect man. So it was decided in the final decision of the nature of the union, at the Council of Chalcedon (A. D. 451), which, after the New Testament, is still, to this day, the highest authority in the Church on this subject. Dr. Huntington may call this a "dramatic union," and flout it as such; nevertheless it *is* the union established by the Church, whose language is : "The difference between the two natures not being destroyed by the union, but rather, the property of each nature being preserved, and concurring in one person and one hypostasis." † If Dr. Huntington rejects the authority of this statement, then he rejects the authority of the Church on this subject. Then he sets up his own opinion, which others indeed may share with him, but which has no authority, against that of the Church. This he has certainly a right to do on Protestant ground, but then he must not appeal to authority.

This statement, it will be seen, precludes the notion that Deity suffered in the supreme Passion. But to

---

* Even the so-called Athanasian Creed explains the union to be "not by confusion of substance, but by unity of person."

† Οὐδαμοῦ τῆς τῶν φύσεων διαφορᾶς ἀνῃρημένης διὰ τὴν ἕνωσιν, σωζομένης δὲ μᾶλλον τῆς ἰδιότητος ἑκατέρας φύσεως, καὶ εἰς ἓν πρόσωπον καὶ μίαν ὑπόστασιν συντρεχούσης.

leave no doubt on the subject, the same Council which decided the nature of the hypostatic union condemned specifically and by name this very doctrine of a suffering God. It was a part of the Eutychian or Monophysite heresy. In fact, the Trinitarian doctrine owes its development in part to the protest of the Christian consciousness against this idea, which seemed to be a necessary corollary of the doctrine of the Monarchians,* and which gave them the *soubriquet* of Patripassians.

Dr. Huntington then is not orthodox in his view of the nature of Christ and the Atonement. We intend no reproach by this assertion, but we think it important for the right apprehension of orthodoxy and the honor of the Church universal, to point out the fact, to define his position in this regard. His doctrine of Christ and the Atonement is not the orthodox doctrine, but one which he sets up for himself on his own responsibility. He is a Eutychian. We do not condemn him in this, we only define him. We condemn no man for any opinion he sincerely holds. But we do condemn the opinion itself as a monstrous invention; we condemn it as a base travesty of the orthodox theory of the Atonement;† we condemn it as, next to "Transubstantiation," the most revolting that was ever propounded within the sphere of the Christian Church. And we charge Dr. Huntington with gross inconsistency in repudiating with such emphasis the idea of a dying God, while advocating that of a suffering one. "God

---

* "Ipsum Patrem passum esse."— Tertull. adv. Praxeam.

† The orthodox theory of the Atonement is the production of St. Anselm, who knows nothing of a suffering God, and indeed lays no stress on *suffering* at all as an element in the Reconciliation.

did not perish : how strange and sad that the thoughtless perversions or wilful misrepresentations of hostile theologians should have made such a statement necessary." * The indignant sorrow expressed in these words strikes us, we must say, as quite out of place. The word *perish* means to pass away, to pass out of sight. No one ever used it as applied to God, in any other sense than that of the putting off of the visible form. And that is precisely what did take place. Surely he who cannot find in the radical idea of Divinity the impossibility of suffering, need never boggle at the word *perish*.

We have touched but few of the errors, as we deem them, of this unfortunate discourse, but have shown enough of error in it to make good our allegation of the inconclusiveness of most of its reasoning, and its misapprehension of the import and bearings of the dogma it defends. The task has not been a pleasant one, but seemed to be due to the cause of that truth to which by profession and name the Christian Examiner is pledged. We regret the publication of the sermon ; it mars the volume that contains it, and does equal injustice to its author and the cause he advocates. No one can estimate that author's real ability more highly than ourselves. But Dr. Huntington is no theologian. His confession might have weight, his reasons have none. If he felt himself impelled by stringent conviction to embrace, and with public confession to espouse the Athanasian faith, and, contenting himself with simple

---

* Page 390.

avowal, had assumed that position, none would have blamed and many would have praised. But in undertaking to expound that faith he has done it a cruel injury, inasmuch as one imprudent and incompetent defender is more injurious than many adversaries. Should he live some ten years longer in the world, — we are sure they will be useful and honorable years, — and continue to grow and seek to inform himself of the matter handled in this discourse, he will also regret its publication and wish to recall it. He will see more plainly than we can point them out its inadequacy and its errors. He will see also that the old doctrine whose new revelation makes him glad and whose new wine inflames him, in whatsoever sense it is true at all, is not the whole truth, and is not the negation, but the complement, of that against which he arrays it. There is a great deal more in it than he now sees, and what is best and deepest in it he does not see, if one may judge his vision by his word.

We shall have failed to make ourselves understood, and shall deem ourselves unfortunate, if in these criticisms we have seemed to impugn the Christian doctrine embodied in the "Trinity." It is only the forced construction of that doctrine in the Constantinopolitan Creed, and the claim that any construction of it, by any council or creed, is of evangelical and binding authority, against which we protest. The belief in the Father, the Son, and the Holy Spirit embraces and œcumenizes Christendom in one confession. The dogma of Tripersonality confuses and divides. The confession is common, the interpretation of it must be left to the individual mind and heart. We would not be supposed to think lightly of its import. To us it is the sum and summit of Christian truth. We see in it that which specifically distinguishes our religion from all antecedent and contemporary faiths, exactly defining it against polytheism on the one hand and Hebrew and Arabian monotheism on the other; evangelically dividing it from Persian dualism on this side and Hindu tritheism on that. We see in it the sublimest and completest theory of God. A God whose nature is neither diffracted by multiplicity nor yet concluded in singularity, who is neither the unconscious All of Pantheism, nor the insulated Self of Judaism; a God whose essence is not to be sought in lone seclusion, but in everlasting self-communication, whose being is a unit and yet a process, — a process of which the two associated names — the Son and the Holy Ghost — are the august terms and the perfect method; a God who allies himself with finite intelligence by the co-eternal, mediating Word, and reflects himself in human nature and enchurches himself in human society by the ever proceeding, sanctifying Spirit. So believing, we also join in the reverent and dear ascription, " Glory be to the Father, and to the Son, and to the Holy Ghost; as it was in the beginning, is now, and ever shall be, world without end! Amen."

PROF. HUNTINGTON'S ARGUMENT FOR THE TRINITY.

[From the Monthly Journal of the Unitarian Association.]

WE propose to examine in this number of our Journal, at some length, the late sermon of Dr. Huntington, in which he gives his reasons for accepting the Doctrine of the Trinity. The title of the sermon is, "Life, Salvation, and Comfort for Man in the Divine Trinity."

When one, who has for twenty years been our companion and friend in preaching the great doctrines of Liberal Christianity, changes his convictions, and leaves us, it would be idle to deny that we feel deep sorrow at his loss. When, as in the present case, he is one of our able ministers, the sorrow is proportionally greater. But, beside this, Dr. Huntington is a man whom we love and esteem for his manliness, earnestness, and Christian fidelity. We shall speak with perfect plainness of the defects in his argument; we shall point out the weakness of his logic; we shall show the root of what we believe to be the great error of his life. But, meantime, we shall try to say all this as we should say it to himself alone.

We believe that "a man can do nothing against the truth," and that all of Prof. Huntington's efforts and abilities are worse than wasted in defending the Church doctrine of the Trinity. If our doctrine is of God, we shall prevail, though all the great men of our body prove apostate. We shall march prospering, though not by their presence. Let them leave us one by one; let them go where the Church is larger, and there is a greater tide of religious sympathy; let them leave our little flock for the great folds. We have a certain compensation for their loss, — a sense of satisfaction in feeling that no foundation is touched, and that our convictions are proved to stand, not in the power of man, but in that of God. There is a double feeling, a complex sentiment; sorrow like that which Jesus felt when many went back, and walked no more with him; but joy like that which led him to bless God that he had hidden these things from the wise and prudent, and revealed them unto babes. As, when Leonidas dismissed from his ranks all but the three hundred, those who were left felt that they could depend on each other; so we, when men whose affinities are only half with the cause of a free and advancing theology retire, can close up our ranks with a certain joy that those at least who remain, and who stand these tests, are surely reliable.

There is no need, then, for apology in examining his sermon, however searching that examination may prove. This is what Dr. Huntington himself must wish. He writes and prints for this purpose, — that we may examine; and thoroughly examine, what he says. But, in order to do this work, it seems most proper to begin by asking why Unitarians reject the doctrine of the Trinity; then we can inquire whether Dr. Huntington has adduced satisfactory answers to these objections, and whether he has brought forward any new statement of the doctrine, or arguments in support of it, which invalidate the Unitarian criticisms of the Church doctrine.

Our course of argument, therefore, will be, —

Briefly to recount the reasons which have induced Unitarians to reject the Trinity.

To see if Dr. Huntington has replied to these reasons.

To examine the positions he has taken, and the arguments by which he supports that position.

The principal reasons, then, for rejecting the Trinity, as assigned by Unitarians, are these: —

1. That it is nowhere taught in the New Testament.

2. That every statement of the Trinity, which has ever been made, has been either (1.) self-contradictory; (2.) unintelligible; (3.) Tritheistic; (4.) or Unitarian, in the form of Sabellianism or of Arianism.

3. That the arguments for it are inadequate.

4. That the arguments against it are overwhelming.

5. That the good ascribed to it does not belong to it, but to the truths which underlie it.

6. That great evils to the Church come from it.

7. That it is a doctrine of philosophy, and not of faith.

8. That we can trace its gradual historic formation in the Christian Church.

9. That it is opposed to a belief in the real Divinity of Christ, and to a belief in his real humanity; thus

undermining continually the faith of the Church in the Divine Humanity of Christ Jesus the Lord.

Proceeding, then, to an examination of these reasons, we say, —

I. The Church doctrine of the Trinity is nowhere stated in the New Testament.

To prove this, as it is a negative proposition, would require us to go through the whole New Testament. But we are saved this necessity by the fact, that we have a statement on this point from one of Dr. Huntington's own witnesses, and one on whom he mainly relies. He brings forward NEANDER, the great Church historian, as a believer in the Trinity (p. 361), and again (p. 378), by an error which he has since candidly admitted, quotes him as saying, "It is the fundamental article of the Christian faith," — which is just what he denies in the following passage. We call Neander to the stand, however, *now*, to have his unimpeachable testimony as a Trinitarian (and a Trinitarian claimed by Dr. Huntington with pride) to the fact, that the doctrine of the Trinity is nowhere stated in the New Testament. This is what Neander says of the Trinity, in the first volume of his great work on Church History (p. 572, Torrey's translation) : —

"We now proceed to the doctrine in which Theism, taken in its connection with the proper and fundamental essence of Christianity or with the doctrine of redemption, finds its ultimate completion, — *the doctrine of the Trinity*. This doctrine does not strictly belong to the fundamental articles of the Christian faith; as appears sufficiently evident from the fact, that *it is expressly held forth in no one particular passage of the New*

Testament: for the only one in which it is done, the passage relating to the three that bear record (1 John v. 7), is undoubtedly spurious, and, in its ungenuine shape, testifies to the fact, how foreign such a collocation is from the style of the New Testament Scriptures. We find in the New Testament no other fundamental article than that of which the Apostle Paul says, that other foundation can no man lay than that is laid, — the annunciation of Jesus as the Messiah."

With this authority we might be content. But Dr. Huntington seems to differ from Neander in thinking that Jesus has himself stated the doctrine of the Trinity, and stated it clearly and fully, in the baptismal formula (Matthew xxviii. 19). He seems to say that this is " a clear and full declaration of the fundamental article of Christian belief." He says, "Now, if ever, Christ will distinctly proclaim the doctrine of Christendom;" and he then declares that Christ in this passage told his Church to baptize " in the Triune name."

Not in the Tri*une* name, certainly. This is an assumption of our friend. He may think that this is implied; that this is to be inferred; that this is what Christ meant: but certainly it is not what Christ said. Christ gives us here *three* objects of baptism, no doubt; but he does not say that they are one. How far this baptismal formula is "a clear and full declaration" of the doctrine of the Trinity will appear thus. The doctrine of the Trinity declares, —

1. That the Father is God.
2. That the Son is God.
3. That the Holy Ghost is God.
4. That the Holy Ghost is a person, like the Father and the Son.

5. That these three persons constitute one God.

Of these five propositions, all of which are essential to the doctrine of the Trinity, *not one is stated in the baptismal formula.* Christ here says *nothing* about the Deity of the Father, the Son, or the Holy Ghost; *nothing* about the personality of either of them; and *nothing* about their Unity. It is difficult to conceive, therefore, how Dr. Huntington can bring himself to call this a command to baptize into the Triune name. We will not refer to his own explanation of Unitarian criticisms, and say, "How desperate the shifts of a determined theory!" because we do not think such an insinuation just or kind. If he chooses to say that his old friends resort to desperate shifts to maintain their theories, because they do not choose to be convinced, he may say so of us: we will not say that of him. Such insinuations, however, we trust, dropped from him in the haste and heat of writing. We do not believe that he intended either bitterness or severity.

Dr. Huntington adds, "Our faith is summoned to the three persons of the one God." But nothing is said of three *persons;* nothing is said of their being one God.

He says, "No hint is given that there is any difference of nature, dignity, duration, power, or glory between them."

We admit it, but also say that no hint is given of any *equality* of nature, dignity, duration, power, or glory between them. Which way, then, is the argument? Christ does not state, on the one hand, that the three are unequal or different; he does not state, on the other hand, that they are equal and the same. The inference of proof from this fact seems to us to be this: If the Apostles, when Christ spoke to them, were already full believers in the Church doctrine of the Trinity, the fact that Christ did not deny it would be an argument in its favor; but if the Apostles were, at that time, wholly ignorant of the Trinity, then the fact that he did not assert it distinctly at least shows that he did not mean to teach it at that time. That inference appears to us a very modest one. But Dr. Huntington will admit that they did not know the doctrine; for he tells us that it was the purpose of Christ to teach it to them at that time. To which we can only reply, If he meant to teach the doctrine, why did he not teach it?

That the *word* TRINITY is not to be found in the New Testament, and that it was invented by Tertullian, is a matter of little consequence; but that the doctrine itself should be nowhere stated in the New Testament, we conceive to be a matter of very great consequence. We have seen that Dr. Huntington's attempt to show that it *is* stated in the baptismal formula is a failure. If not stated there, we presume that he will not maintain that it is stated anywhere. We therefore agree with Neander in saying, that, whether the doctrine be true or not, it is not taught distinctly in the New Testament. If taught at all, it is only taught inferentially; that is, it is a matter of reasoning, not a matter of faith. It is metaphysics: it is not religion.

II. The second reason why Unitarians reject the Church doctrine of the Trinity is this:—

That every statement of the Trinity has proved, on examination, to be either (1.) a contradiction in terms, or (2.) unintelligible, or (3.) Tritheistic, or (4.) Unitarianism under a Trinitarian form.

Let us examine this objection. What is the general statement of the Trinity, as made by the Orthodox Church, Catholic and Protestant? Fortunately this question is easily answered.

Orthodoxy has been consistent since the Middle Ages in its general statement, however much it may have varied in its explanations of what it meant by that statement.

(1.) *Contradiction in Terms.*

The doctrine of the Trinity, as it stands in the creeds of the churches, is this: —

There is in the nature of God three persons, — the Father, the Son, and the Holy Ghost; and these three are one being. They are the same in substance, equal in power and glory. Each of these three persons is very God, infinite in all attributes; and yet there are not three Gods, but one God.

According to the general doctrine of Orthodoxy, the unity of God is in being, essence, and substance; that is, God is one being, God is one essence, God is one substance. The threefold division stops short of the being of God: it does not penetrate to his essential nature; it does not divide his substance.

What, then, is the Trinity? It is a Trinity of persons.

But what is meant by "person," as used in this doctrine? According to the common and familiar use of the word at the present time, three persons are three beings. Personality expresses the most individual existence imaginable. If, therefore, the word "person" is to be taken according to the common use of the phrase, the doctrine of the Trinity would be evidently a contradiction in terms. It would be equivalent to saying, God is one being, but God is three beings; which again would be equivalent to saying that one is three.

Now, Trinitarians generally are too acute and clear-sighted to fall into such a palpable contradiction as this. It is a common accusation against them, that they believe one to be three, and three one; but this charge is, in most cases, unjust. This would be only true in case they affirmed that God is three in the same way in which he is one; but they do not usually say this. They declare that he is one being, — not three beings. They declare that the threefold distinction relates to personality, not to being; and that they use the word "person," not in the common sense, but in a peculiar sense, to express, as well as they can, a distinction, which, from the poverty of language, no word can be found to express exactly. Thus St. Augustine confessed, long ago, "We say that there are three persons, not in order to say anything, but in order not to be wholly silent." *Non ut aliquid diceretur, sed ut ne taceretur.* And so Archbishop Whately, in the notes to his Logic, regrets that the word "person" should ever have been used by our divines; and says, "If *hypostasis*, or any other completely foreign word, had been used instead, no idea at all would have been conveyed, except that of the explanation given; and thus the danger, at least, of being misled by a word, would have been avoided."

(2.) *The Unintelligible Statement.*

The Trinitarian thus avoids asking us to believe a contradiction: but in avoiding this, he runs upon another rock, — that, namely, of not asking us to believe anything at all; for if "person" here does *not* mean what it commonly means, and if it be impossible, from the poverty of language, to define precisely the idea which is intended by it, we are then asked to believe a proposition which Trinitarians themselves are unable to express. But a proposition which is not expressed is no proposition. A proposition, any important term of which is unintelligible, is wholly unintelligible.

To make this matter clear, let us put it into a conversational form. We will suppose that two persons meet together, — one a Unitarian, the other a Trinitarian.

Trinitarian. You do not believe the Trinity? Then you cannot be saved. No one can be saved who denies the Trinity. It is a vital and fundamental doctrine.

Unitarian. Tell me what it is, and I will see if I can believe it. What is the Trinity?

Trin. God exists as one being, but three persons.

Unit. What do you mean by "person"? Do you mean a person like Peter, James, or John?

Trin. No: we use "person" from the poverty of language. We do not mean that.

Unit. What, then, do you mean by it?

Trin. It is a mystery. We cannot understand it precisely.

Unit. I have no objection to the doctrine being mysterious; I believe a great many things which are mysterious: but I don't want the *language* to be mysterious. You might as well use a Greek or a Hebrew or a Chinese word, and ask me to believe that there are three *hypostases* or three *prosopa* in Deity, if you do not tell me what you mean by the word "person."

Trin. It is a great mystery. It is a matter of *faith*, not of *reasoning*. You must believe it, and not speculate about it.

Unit. Believe *it?* Believe *what?* I am waiting for you to tell me what I am to believe. I am ready to exercise my faith; but you are tasking, not my faith, but my knowledge of language. I suppose that you do not wish me to believe *words*, but thoughts. I wish to look through the word and see what thought lies behind it.

Now, it seems to us that this is a very fair demand of the Unitarian. To ask us to believe a proposition, any important term of which is unintelligible, is precisely equivalent to asking us to believe no proposition at all. Let us listen to Paul: "Even things without life, giving sound, whether pipe or harp, except they give a distinction in the sounds, how shall it be known what is piped or harped? For, if the trumpet give an uncertain sound, who shall prepare himself for battle? So likewise ye, except ye utter by the tongue words easy to be understood, — how shall it be known what is spoken? *for ye shall speak into the air.* . . . For, if I know not the meaning of the voice, I shall be unto him that speaketh a Barbarian; and he that speaketh, a Barbarian unto me."

It is of no use to talk about mystery in order to excuse ourselves for not using intelligible language. That which is *mysterious* is one thing: that which is *unintelligible* is quite another thing. We may understand what a mystery is, thought we cannot comprehend *how* it is; but that which is unintelligible we neither comprehend nor understand at all. We neither know *how* it is nor *what* it is. Thus, for example, the fact of God's foreknowledge and man's freedom is a mystery. I cannot comprehend how God can foreknow what I am to do to-morrow, and yet I be free to do it or not do it. I cannot comprehend how Jesus should be delivered to death by the determined counsel and foreknowledge of God, and yet the Jews have been free agents in crucifying him, and accountable for it. These things are mysteries; but they are not unintelligible as doctrines. I see what is meant by them. There is no obscurity in the assertion that God foreknows everything; nor in the other assertion, that man is a free agent. I can see clearly what is implied *in both statements*, although my mind cannot grasp both, and bring them together, and show the way in which they may be reconciled. So, too, infinity is a mystery. We cannot comprehend it. Our mind cannot go round it, grasp it, sustain it. Our thought sinks baffled before the attempt to penetrate to the depth of such a wonderful idea. But we understand well enough what is meant by infinity. There is nothing obscure in *the statement* of the fact that the universe is unbounded. So the way in which a flower grows from its seed is mysterious. We cannot comprehend how the wonderful principle of life can be wrapped up in those little folds, and how it can cause the root to strike downward, and the airy stalk to spring lightly upward, and the leaves to unfold, and, last of all, the bright, consummate flower to open its many-colored eye. But certainly we can understand very well *the statement* that a flower grows, though we do not comprehend how it grows.

Do not, then, tell us, when you have announced a

doctrine, the language of which is unintelligible, that you have told us a mystery. You have done no such thing. Your proposition is not mysterious: it is unintelligible. It is not a mystery: it is only a mystification.

(3.) *The Tritheistic Statement.*

Leaving, then, this ground of mystery, and attempting to define more clearly what he means by three persons and one substance, the Trinitarian often sinks the Unity in the Triplicity, and so runs ashore upon Tritheism. This happens when he explains the term "person" as implying independent existence; in which case the Unity is changed into Union. Then we have really three Gods: the FATHER, who devises the plan of redemption; the SON, who goes forth to execute it; and the HOLY SPIRIT, who sanctifies believers. If there are these three distinct beings, they can be called one God only as they are one in will, in aim, in purpose, — only as they agree perfectly on all points. The Unity of God, then, becomes only a unity of agreement, not a unity of being. This is evidently not the Unity which is taught in the Bible, where Jesus declares that the *first of all the commandments is*, "Hear, O Israel! the Lord our God is ONE Lord."

Moreover, against such a Trinity as this there are insuperable objections, from grounds of reason as well as of Scripture. For God is the Supreme Being, the Most High; and how can there be *three* Supreme Beings, three Most High Gods? Again: God is the first cause; but if the Father, the Son, and the Holy Ghost are each God, and all equal in power and majesty, and have each an independent existence, then there are three first causes; which is evidently impossible. Again: one of the attributes of God is his independent or absolute existence. A being who depends on another cannot be the Supreme God. The Father, Son, and Spirit, therefore, cannot depend on each other; for each, by depending on another, would cease to be the independent God. But if they do not depend on each other, then each ceases to be God, who is the First Cause; for that being is not the first cause who has two other beings independent of him. Other arguments of the same kind might be adduced to show that there cannot be three necessary beings. In fact, all the arguments from reason, which go to prove the Unity of God, prove a unity of nature, not of agreement.

"But why argue against Tritheism?" you may say. "Are any Tritheists?" Yes: many Trinitarians are in reality Tritheists, by their own account of themselves. There are many who make the *Unity* of God a mere unity of agreement, and talk about the *society* in the Godhead, and the *intercourse* between the Father, Son, and Spirit.*

---

* Dr. Horace Bushnell, a favorite authority with Prof. Huntington, whom Prof. Huntington quotes largely, and whose views he earnestly recommends, gives us his testimony to this point, thus ("God in Christ," pp. 130, 131):—

"A very large portion of Christian teachers, together with the general mass of disciples, undoubtedly hold three real living persons in the interior nature of God; that is, three consciousnesses, wills, hearts, understandings."

"*A very large portion of Christian teachers*" hold, then, to a belief in three Gods; and with them is joined "*the general mass of the disciples.*" The only Unity held by these teachers is, he goes

Opposed to this kind of Trinity is another view, in which the Unity is preserved, but the Trinity lost. According to this view, God is one Being, who reveals himself in three ways,—as Father, as Son, as Spirit, —or sustains three relations, or manifests himself in three modes of operation. The Trinity here becomes a nominal thing, and is, in reality, only Unitarianism with an Orthodox name. This kind of Trinity also is very prevalent, and is the only one really maintained by men of high standing in the Orthodox Church, both in Europe and America. According to this view, the word "person" in the doctrine of the Trinity means the same as the corresponding word in Greek and Latin formerly meant; namely, the outward character, not the inward individuality. Thus Cicero says, "I, being one, sustain three persons or characters; my own, that of my client, and that of the judge,"—*Ego unus, sustineo tres personas.*

This view of the Trinity is commonly called Modalism, or Sabellianism; and is also widely held by those who call themselves Trinitarians. It is, in fact, only Unitarianism under a Trinitarian name.*

---

on to say, "a social Unity." Father, Son, and Holy Ghost are, in their view, socially united only; and preside in that way, as a kind of celestial Tritheocracy, over the world. This heresy, he says, "because of its clear opposition to Unitarianism, is counted safe, and never treated as a heresy." That is, the Christian Church allows the belief in *three Gods*, and will not discipline those who hold that opinion; but, if you believe strictly and only in *one God*, you cannot be saved!

* Dr. Bushnell goes on to say (p. 133), "While the Unity is thus confused and lost in the threeness, perhaps I should admit that the threeness sometimes appears to be clouded or obscured

(4.) *The Subordination View.*

Avoiding these two extremes, and yet wishing to retain a distinct idea of Unity and Tripersonality, the Trinitarian is necessarily driven upon a third view, in which the Father is the only really Supreme and Independent Being, the Son and the Holy Spirit subordinate and dependent.

This view, which is called the subordination scheme, or Arianism, is Unitarianism again in another form; and this view also is entertained by many who still retain the name of "Trinitarians." According to this view, the Son and the Holy Ghost are really God, but are so by a derived divinity. God the Father communicates his divinity to the Son and the Holy Ghost. This is the view really taken in the Nicene Creed, though adopted in opposition to the Arians; and was the doctrine of the earliest Church Fathers before the Arian controversy began. In the Nicene Creed, we read that the Son is " God of ($\dot{\epsilon}\kappa$) God, Light of ($\dot{\epsilon}\kappa$) Light, true God of true God;" the "*of*" here being the same as "from," and denoting origin and derivation.

---

by the Unity. Thus it is sometimes protested, that in the word 'person' nothing is meant beyond a threefold distinction; though it will always be observed, that nothing is really meant by the protestation; that the protester goes on to speak and to reason of the three, not as being only somewhats or distinctions, but as metaphysical and real persons. . . . . Indeed, it is a somewhat curious fact in theology, that the class of teachers who protest over the word 'person,' declaring that they mean only a *threefold distinction*, cannot show that there is really a hair's breadth of difference between their doctrine and the doctrine asserted by many of the later Unitarians."

This doctrine seems, in reality, to have less in its favor than either of the others. By calling the Son and Holy Spirit God, it contrives to make three distinct Gods, and so is Tritheism; and yet, by making them dependent on the Father, it becomes Unitarianism again. Thus, singularly enough, this attempt at making a compromise between Unity and Trinity loses both Unity and Trinity: for it makes three Gods, and so loses the Unity; and yet it makes Christ not "God over all," not the Supreme Being, and so loses the Trinity.

Between these different views, between Tritheism, Sabellianism, and Arianism, the Orthodox Trinity has always swung to and fro, — inclining more to one or to the other, according to the state of controversy in any particular age. When the Arian or Tritheistic views were proclaimed and defended, the Orthodoxy of the Church swung over towards Sabellianism, making the Unity strong and solid; and the Trinity became a thin mode or an airy abstraction. When Sabellianism, thus encouraged, came openly forward, and defended its system and won adherents, then Church Orthodoxy would hasten to set up barriers on that side, and would fall back upon Tritheistic ground, making the Threefold Personality a profound and real distinction, penetrating the very nature of Deity, and changing the Unity of Being into a mere Unity of Will or agreement. We will venture to say, that there has never yet been a definition of the Trinity which has not been either Tritheistic or Modalistic; and Church Orthodoxy has always stood either on Tritheistic or on Sabellian ground. In other words, the Orthodox Trinity of any age, when searched to the bottom, has proved to be Unitarianism after all, — Unitarianism in the Tritheistic or in the Sabellian disguise; for the Tritheism of three co-equal, independent, and absolute Gods is too much opposed both to reason and Scripture to be able ever to maintain itself openly as a theology for any length of time.

The analogies which are used to explain the Trinity are all either Sabellian or Tritheistic. Nature has been searched in all ages for these analogies, by which to make the Trinity plain; but none have ever been found which did not make the Trinity either Sabellianism or Tritheism. They are either three parts of the substance, or else three qualities or modes of the substance.

Thus we have instances in which the three are made the three parts of one being, or substance; as in *man*, — spirit, soul, body; thought, affection, will; head, heart, hand.

One Being with three distinct faculties is Tritheism: one Being acting in three directions is Sabellianism.

Time is past, present, and future. Syllogism has its major, minor, and conclusion. There are other like analogies.

St. Patrick took for his illustration the three leaves of trefoil or clover. Others have imagined the Trinity like a triangle; or they have referred to the three qualities of space, — height, breadth, width; or of fire, — form, light, and heat; or of a noun, which has its masculine, feminine, and neuter; or of a government, consisting of king, lords, and commons, or of executive, legislative, and judiciary.

This survey of Church Trinity shows that it is either one in which, —

1. The persons are not defined; or an unintelligible Trinity.

2. Or which defines person and Unity in the usual sense; or a contradictory Trinity.

3. Or which defines person as usual, and the Unity as only Union; or Tritheism.

4. Or which defines person as only manifestation; or Sabellianism.

These four are all the views ever hitherto given, and are all untenable. We might stop here, and say that the Trinity is utterly unsupported. There is no need of going to the Scripture to see if it is taught there; for we have, as yet, nothing to look for in Scripture.

The Trinitarian's difficulty appears to be in defining person. But possibly he may say, "I cannot, indeed, give a positive idea of person; but I can give a *negative* one. I cannot say what it *is;* but I can say what it is *not*. It is *not* a mere *mode*, on the one hand; and not *being*, on the other. We must neither confound the persons nor divide the substance."

We will, then, go further, and say, as Trinitarians have never yet defined person, without making it either a mode or a being, so they never can define it otherwise. There is no third between being and mode. They *must* either confound the persons or divide the substance.

Again: that which differences one person in the Deity from another must be either a perfection or an imperfection. There is nothing between these. But it cannot be an imperfection; for no imperfection exists in God: and it cannot be a perfection; for then the other two persons would want a divine perfection, and would be imperfect.

III. The arguments in support of the Trinity are wholly inadequate. Since, according to Neander, the Trinity is not stated in the New Testament, it follows that it is a doctrine of *inference* only; that is, a piece of human reasoning. Now, we have, no doubt, a perfect right to infer doctrines from Scripture which are not stated there; but, as Protestants, we have no right to make these inferences fundamental, or essential to the religious life. They may, indeed, be metaphysically essential; that is, essential to a well-arranged system: but they are not morally essential; that is, not essential to the moral and spiritual life of the soul.

But this is just what Prof. Huntington attempts to do. He tries to show that there is a doctrine essential to the life, peace, and progress of man, which the New Testament has omitted to state; which is neither distinctly stated by our Saviour nor by any of his Apostles; which has been left to be inferred, and inferred by the mere processes of unaided human reason.

What arguments does he allege for this?

His first and principal argument is the *universal belief of the Christian Church in the doctrine of the Trinity.*

On this, Prof. Huntington lays great stress. He says:—

"Truth is not determined by majorities; and yet it would be contrary to the laws of our constitution not to be affected by a testimony so vast, uniform, and sacred as that which is rendered by the common belief of Christian history and the Christian countries to the truth of the Trinity. There is something extremely painful, not to say irreverent, towards the Providence which has watched and led the true Christian Israel, in presuming that a tenet so emphatically and gladly received in all the ages and regions of Christendom as almost literally to meet the terms of the test of Vincentius, — Believed always, everywhere, and by all, — is unfounded in revelation and truth. Such a conclusion puts an aspect of uncertainty over the mind of the Church, scarcely consistent with any tolerable confidence in that great promise of the Master, that he would be with his own all days." — p. 359.

To which we answer, —

(1.) That, according to Dr. Bushnell (Mr. Huntington's own witness), there never has been, nor is now, any such belief in the doctrine of the Trinity as he asserts. The larger part of the Church have always "divided the substance" of the Deity, and another large portion have "confounded the persons;" and so the majority of the Church, while holding the word "Trinity," have never believed in the Tri-unity at all.

Prof. Huntington summons Dr. Bushnell as a witness to the practical value of the Trinity; and we may suppose something such an examination as this to take place : —

Prof. Huntington. Tell us, Dr. Bushnell, what instances you know of persons who have been converted or deeply blessed by the holy doctrine of the Trinity.

Dr. Bushnell. I have known of "a great cloud of witnesses," "living myriads," "who have been raised to a participation of God in the faith of this adorable mystery." (Huntington, p. 413.)

Prof. H. Mention some of them.

Dr. B. "Francis Junius," "two centuries and a half ago,"—a Professor "at Heidelberg [Leyden?], testified that he was, in fact, converted from atheism by the Christian Trinity;" also "the mild and sober Howe;" "Jeremy Taylor;" also "the Marquis de Rentz," "Edwards," and "Lady Maxwell." (Huntington, p. 414.)

Unitarian. Say, Dr. Bushnell, whether, in your opinion, the majority of Christians really believe in the Church doctrine of the Trinity.

Dr. B. "A very large portion of the Christian teachers, together with the general mass of disciples, undoubtedly hold three living persons in the interior nature of God." (Bushnell, "God in Christ," p. 130.)

Unit. Is that Scriptural or Orthodox?

Dr. B. No. It is only "a social Unity." It is "a celestial Tritheocracy." It "boldly renounces Orthodoxy at the point opposite to Unitarianism." (*Ibid.*, p. 131.)

Unit. Do I understand you to be now speaking of the properly Orthodox ministers and churches generally?

Dr. B. "Our properly Orthodox teachers and churches, while professing three persons, also retain the verbal profession of one person. They suppose themselves really to hold that God is one person: and yet they most certainly do not; they only confuse their understanding, and call their confusion faith. This I affirm on the ground of sufficient evidence; partly because it cannot be otherwise, and partly because it visibly is not." (*Ibid.*, p. 131.)

Unit. Do you believe, Dr. Bushnell, that spiritual good can come from such a belief in the Trinity as you describe to be "undoubtedly" that of "the general mass of disciples"?

Dr. B. "Mournful evidence will be found that a confused and painfully bewildered state is often produced by it. They are practically at work in their thoughts to choose between the three; sometimes actually and decidedly preferring one to another; doubting how to adjust their mind in worship; uncertain, after, which of the three to obey; turning away, possibly, from one with a feeling of dread that might well be called aversion; devoting themselves to another as the Romanist to his patron saint. This, in fact, is Polytheism, and not the clear, simple love of God. There is true love in it, doubtless; but the comfort of love is not here. The mind is involved in a dismal confusion, which we cannot think of without the sincerest pity. No soul can truly rest in God, when God is in two or three, and these in such a sense that a choice between them must be continually suggested." (*Ibid.*, p. 134.)

Unit. This state of mind is that of undoubtedly the general mass of the disciples?

Dr. B. It is. (*Ibid.*, p. 130.)

Unit. Are there others, calling themselves Trinitarians, who hold essentially the Unitarian doctrine?

Dr. B. Yes. "It is a somewhat curious fact in theology, that the class of teachers who protest over the word 'person,' declaring that they mean only a *threefold distinction*, cannot show that there is really a hair's breadth of difference between their doctrine and the doctrine asserted by many of the later Unitarians. They may teach or preach in a very different manner; they probably do: but the theoretic contents of their opinion cannot be distinguished. Thus, they say that there is a certain divine person in the man Jesus Christ; but that, when they use the term 'person,' they mean, not a person, but a certain indefinite and indefinable distinction. The later Unitarians, meantime, are found asserting that God is present in Christ in a mysterious and peculiar communication of his being; so that he is the living embodiment and express image of God. If, now, the question be raised, 'Wherein does the indefinable *distinction* of one differ from the mysterious and peculiar *communication* of the other?' or, 'How does it appear that there is any difference?' there is no living man, I am quite sure, who can invent an answer." (*Ibid.*, p. 135.)

Unit. Is it not true that both of these views are sometimes held alternately by Trinitarians?

Dr. B. "Probably there is a degree of alternation, or inclining from one side to the other, in this view of Trinity, as the mind struggles, now to embrace one, and now the other, of two incompatible notions. Some persons are more habitually inclined to hold the three; a very much smaller number, to hold the one." (*Ibid.*, p. 134.)

Unit. But can they not hold the Unity with this Trinity?

Dr. B. "No man can assert three persons, meaning three consciousnesses, wills, and understandings, and still have any intelligent meaning in his mind, when he asserts that they are yet one person. For, as he now uses the term, the very idea of a person is that of an essential, incommunicable monad, bounded by consciousness, and vitalized by self-active will; which being true, he might as well profess to hold that three units are yet one unit. When he does it, his words will, of necessity, be only substitutes for sense." (*Ibid.,* p. 131.)

(2.) But suppose that the belief of the Church in the Trinity was as universal as Prof. Huntington asserts and Dr. Bushnell denies, what would be its value? His argument proves too much. If it proves the Trinity to be true, it proves, *à fortiori,* the Roman Catholic Church to be the true Church, and Protestantism to be an error; for Martin Luther, at one time, was the only Protestant in the world. Suppose that a Roman priest had come to him then. He might have addressed Luther thus: —

"It is certainly an impressive testimony to the truth of the Church of Rome, that the Christian world have been so generally agreed in it. Truth is not determined by majorities; and yet it would be contrary to the laws of our constitution not to be affected by a testimony so vast, uniform, and sacred as that which is rendered by the common belief of Christian history and the Christian countries to the doctrines and practices of the Roman Catholic Church. We travel abroad, through these converted lands, over the round world. We enter, at the call of the Sabbath morning light, the place of assembled worshippers; let it be the newly planted conventicle on the edge of the Western forest, or the missionary station at the extremity of the Eastern continent; let it be the collection of Northern mountaineers, or of the dwellers in Southern valleys; let it be in the plain village meeting-house, or in the magnificent cathedrals of the old cities; let it be the crowded congregation of the metropolis, or the 'two or three' that meet in faith in upper chambers, in log-huts, or under palm-trees; let it be regenerate bands gathered to pray in the islands of the ocean, or thankful circles of believers confessing their dependence and beseeching pardon on ships' decks, in the midst of the ocean. So we pass over the outstretched countries of both hemispheres; and it is well-nigh certain — so certain that the rare and scattered exceptions drop out of the broad and general conclusion — that the lowly petitions, the fervent supplications, the hearty confessions, the eager thanksgivings, or the grand peals of choral adoration, which our ears will hear, will be uttered according to the grand ritual of the Church of Rome. This is the voice of the unhesitating praise that embraces and hallows the globe."

What would Luther have replied to that? He would have said: "Truth must have a beginning. It is always, at first, in a minority. The gate of it is strait, the path to it narrow, and few find it. All reforms are, at the beginning, in the hands of a small number. If God and truth are on our side, what do we care for your multitudes?" We can make the same answer now.

Prof. Huntington proceeds to give his own creed in regard to the Trinity, — to state his own belief.

God, in himself, he declares, we cannot know at all. We know him only in his revelation. "Out of that ineffable and veiled Godhead — the groundwork, if we may say so, of all divine manifestation (or theophany), there emerge to us, in revelation, the three whom we rightly call persons, — Father, Son, and Holy Ghost."

We can only conceive of God, he says, in action; and in action we behold him as three. But action and revelation take place in time. The Trinity, therefore, according to Prof. Huntington, is only known to us in temporal manifestation; whether it exists in eternity or not, we cannot tell. And yet, in the next sentence, he goes on to say that "the Son is eternally begotten of the Father," and "the Holy Ghost proceeds out of the Father, *not in time:*" which is the very thing he had a moment before professed to know nothing about. It is very difficult, therefore, to tell precisely what his view is. With regard to the incarnation of the Son he is still more obscure. He says that "Christ comes forth out of the Godhead as the Son;" that he "leaves the glory he had with the Father;" that, while he is on earth, the Father alone represents the unseen personality of the Godhead, and that therefore the Son appears to be dependent on him, and submissive; that temporarily, while the Son is in the world, he remains ignorant of what the Father knows, and says that his Father is greater than he. "He lessens himself to dependency for the sake of mediation." — "All this we might expect." This he calls an "instrumental inequality between Son and Father:" it "is wrought into the Biblical language; remains in all our devotional habit, and ought to remain there."

In other words, Prof. Huntington believes that the Infinite God became less than infinite in the incarnation. The common explanation of those passages where Christ says, for example, "My Father is greater than I," does not satisfy him. He is not satisfied that Jesus said it "in his human nature." No; it was the divine nature which said it; and it was really GOD THE SON, who did not know the day nor the hour of his own coming. He lost a part of his omniscience. He ceased to be perfect in all his attributes. We should say, then, that he ceased to be God: but Prof. Huntington maintains that he was God, nevertheless; but God less than omnipotent, — God less than omniscient; God the Son, so distinct from the Father as to be ignorant of what the Father knew, and unable to perform what the Father could do.

Prof. Huntington seems to be aware that some objection may be taken to this view, and so goes on to suggest that all such objections will proceed from an unspiritual nature; and he intimates that no answer nor any criticism will disturb him at all. "I know in whom I have believed," will be reply enough to all objections.

Very well, we say: matters of faith are matters of faith, and to be spiritually discerned; but matters of opinion belong to the intellect, and are to be intellectually discerned. You come to us, Prof. Huntington, your old friends, who think just as you thought yourself, when, a few years since, you gave seven reasons for not believing the Trinity, — you come to us, and call on us to believe it. "Believe what?" — "The Trinity." — "Well, what particular view of the Trinity? Tell us what it is." He then proceeds to make his statement: "*This is the* Trinity you are to believe." We produce our objections to his particular view: whereupon he suddenly retires behind a cloud of glowing religious rhetoric, recites to us a passage from the First Corinthians, and tells us plainly that we have no spiritual insight; that we are in danger of "cold and extreme negatives;" that we have "too much conscious complacency in our supposed originality;" but that he "knows in whom he has believed."

Prof. Huntington (p. 366) ascribes it to "condescension" in Christ, to say that "of that day and hour knoweth not the Son." — "*It is condescension indeed!*" says he. But this word "condescension" does not well apply here. One does not condescend to be ignorant of what he knows: still less does a truthful person condescend *to say* he is ignorant of what he knows. We may wisely condescend to help the feeble, and sympathize with the lowly, but hardly to be ignorant with them, or to pretend to be ignorant. It is a badly chosen word, and seems to show the vacillation of the writer's thought.

IV. The arguments against the doctrine of the Trinity are unanswerable.

We infer that they are unanswerable from the fact that they are not answered. It is to be presumed that Prof. Huntington, having been for so many years a preacher of Unitarian doctrine, is acquainted with our arguments. It is a remarkable fact, that, in this sermon, he has nowhere attempted to reply to them. He has passed them wholly by. You would not know, from reading the discourse, that he had ever been a Unitarian, or had ever heard of the Unitarian objections to the Trinity; still less that he had himself preached against it. Unitarians, for instance, have said, that *if the Trinity be true, and if it be so important to the welfare of the soul as is contended, it would be somewhere plainly taught in the New Testament.* Does Prof.

Huntington answer this argument? No: he answers the argument from the *word* "Trinity" not being in the Bible, and his answer is sufficient; but he does not answer the argument from the fact, that the doctrine itself is not anywhere distinctly taught, and that none of the terms which have been found essential to any Orthodox statement of the doctrine are to be met with in the New Testament.*

Nor does Prof. Huntington anywhere fairly meet the Unitarian argument from the impossibility of stating the doctrine in intelligible language. He tells us, with his usual eloquence, what we have often enough been told before, that there are many things which we do not understand, and that we must believe many facts the *mode* of which is unintelligible. But when we say, "Can we believe *a doctrine* or proposition which cannot be distinctly stated?" he has no answer. The Trinity is *a doctrine*, and must therefore be distinctly stated in order to be believed. It has not been distinctly stated,† and therefore cannot be believed. To this objection, Prof. Huntington has no reply; and we may conclude that it is an unanswerable objection.

Dr. Huntington uses an unnecessary phrase about those who object to mystery. He calls the objection

---

* "It has often been asserted *and admitted*," says Twesten, one of the strongest of modern Trinitarians, "that even the principal notions about which the Church doctrine turns are foreign to the New Testament; as οὐσία and ὑπόστασις, τρόπος ὑπάρξεως and ἀποκαλύψεως, τριάς and ὁμοούσια." (Twesten, "Dogmatik," Vol. II. p. 281.)

† "Who will venture to say that any of the definitions heretofore given of personality in the Godhead, in itself considered, —

"shallow self-illusion," and proceeds with the usual declaration, that all of life is mysterious. Can he have been a Unitarian preacher for twenty years, and not have known that Unitarians object to mystery only when it is used by Trinitarians as a cover for obscurity and vagueness of statement?

You ask us to believe a precise statement; viz. that "there are three *persons* in the Godhead." We say, "What do you mean by 'person'?" The Trinitarian answers, "It is a mystery." We say, "We cannot believe it, then." The Trinitarian replies, "Why, all is a mystery. How the grass grows is a mystery; yet you believe it." — "No," we say, "we do not believe it. When the mystery begins, our belief ends: we believe up to that point, and no further." The statement, "the grass grows," is *not* a mystery: the fact, "the grass grows," is *not* a mystery. We believe the fact and the statement. The *way* in which it grows *is* mysterious; and we do not believe anything about it. "You cannot understand *how* the grass grows." No; and, accordingly, we do not believe anything about *how* the grass grows. But the whole purpose of the Trinity is to show *how* the Father, the Son, and the Holy Spirit exist. You are not satisfied that we receive *what* the Scripture teaches: you try to show us the *how*, and then leave it in obscurity at last.

---

such definitions as have their basis in the Nicene or Athanasian Creed, — are intelligible and satisfactory to the mind? At least, I can truly say, that I have not been able to find them, if they do in fact exist; nor, so far as I know, has any one been able, by any commentary on them, to make them clear and satisfactory." (Prof. Stuart, "Biblical Repository," April, 1835. See Wilson, "Trin. Test.," p. 272.)

Nor does Dr. Huntington reply to the Unitarian explanation of the Trinitarian proof-texts. Trinitarians have often quoted the texts, "*I and my Father are one;*" "*He who has seen me has seen the Father,*" — in proof of the Deity of Christ. Unitarians have often replied to both of them: to the first passage, that since Jesus has also said that his *disciples were to be one with him, as he is one with God*, it either proves that the disciples are also to be God, or does *not* prove that Christ is God. To the second passage, Unitarians have replied by reading the next clause, in which Christ says, "Believest thou not that I am *in* the Father?" showing how it is that he reveals the Father. He is *in* the Father, and his disciples are *in* him. Those who see him, see the Father: those who see his true disciples, see the face and image of Christ. These answers are so obvious, and Prof. Huntington must have heard them so often, that he should, as a controversialist, have taken some notice of them. He has not done so.

He quotes the passage from Eph. i. 20, 21; and says, "*Can this be a creature?*" We reply, Can he be anything *but* a creature? — he who was *set* by God in this place of honor. Does God *set* God, as a reward, above principalities and powers? Does God make God "head over all things in the Church"? Again: Prof. Huntington quotes, "That, at the name of Jesus, every knee should bow, and every tongue confess that he is Lord;" but he omits the conclusion, "to the glory of God the Father."

He even quotes the passage, "Him *hath God exalted* to give repentance and forgiveness of sin."

And he quotes the passage, which has staggered the strongest believers in the Trinity, where Paul declares (1 Cor. xv.), that, *at the end*, Christ will give up his kingdom to the Father, that "God may be all in all," and explains it as meaning that "he will resume his place in the coequal Three, the indivisible One." Has he *left* his place, then? Is that Orthodox? Prof. Huntington evidently thinks so; for he says, "The Son, in his character of Sonship, is retaken, so to speak, into the everlasting undivided One." *So to speak.* We may *speak* so: "But what do we mean by it?" is the question. Did God the Son leave his place in the Godhead? did he become less than God? did he become ignorant? did he suffer and die? did he arise, and at last re-ascend, and take his place, "so to speak," in the Godhead? If this is meant as real statement, what better is it than the Avatars of Vishnu? What sort of Unity is left to us? We have a Trinity of council; but where is the Unity, except of agreement? One Divine Being descending, and leaving the other Divine Being alone, temporarily, on the throne of the universe, until the Divine Being who had descended should re-ascend to take his seat again "in the coequal Three and indivisible One"!

One Unitarian argument, which appears to us unanswerable, is in the fact, that the very passages in which the highest attributes are ascribed to Christ are always those in which his dependence and subordination are most strongly asserted. We could throw aside all the passages in which Jesus asserts directly his inferiority, — as, "My Father is greater than I;" "Of mine own self I can do nothing," — and take the strongest proof-texts of the Trinitarians, and ask for no better proof for the Unitarian doctrine: "All power is given to me in heaven and earth;" "The image of the invisible God, the first-born of every creature;" "In him dwelt all the fulness of the Godhead bodily." Are these passages written of Christ in his divine or human nature? Not his divine nature; for to God the Son all power cannot be "given." God the Son cannot be "the image of God," or the "first-born of every *creature.*" The "fulness of the Godhead" cannot dwell in God the Son. They must, then, be said of him in his human nature; and, if so, they show that the loftiest titles and attributes do not prove him to be God.

V. The good ascribed to the doctrine of the Trinity does not belong to it, but to the truths which underlie it.

Dr. Huntington asserts, for example, that "the Trinity of God appears to be the necessary means of manifesting and supporting, in the mind of our race, a faith in the true personality of God."

If so, it is remarkable that the two forms of religion in which the personality of God, as absolute will, is most distinctly recognized (i. e. the *Jewish* religion and the *Mohammedan* religion), should both be ignorant of the Trinity. It is equally remarkable that the most Pantheistic religion in the world, in which the personality of God most entirely disappears (i. e. Braminism), should have a Trinity of its own. It is also remarkable, on this hypothesis, that idolatry in the Christian Church (as worship of Mary, worship of saints and relics, &c.) should come up with the Trinity, and flourish simultaneously with it.

No: it is not the Trinity which brings out most distinctly the personality of God, but the faith in a divine revelation through inspired men. If God can dwell in the souls of men, teaching and guiding them, he must be a person like the soul with which he communes. Especially does the religious consciousness of Jesús, his simple and childlike communion with the Heavenly Father, bring God near to the soul as a personal being. It is not the Trinity, but the Christian faith which underlies it, which teaches the divine personality.

Nor is it the doctrine of the Trinity which is necessary for a living faith in God through Christ, reconciling the world unto himself. All that Dr. Huntington says of the evil of sin is well said, but has no bearing on the point before us. According to Prof. Huntington's own witnesses, as we have seen above, the Trinity was unknown in the earlier ages of the Church. Was reconciliation unknown? Was the forgiving love of Christ unknown? If he cannot assert this, the doctrine of the Trinity is not necessary to a living faith in a reconciling God.

Prof. Huntington argues, that only the sufferings, and actual sufferings, of God himself, can touch the sinful heart; and, therefore, the Trinity is true. The conclusion is a long way from the premise, even supposing that to be sound. But as regards the premise: he has read and quoted Mansell. Has he not verged toward the dogmatism which that writer condemns? Would it not be more modest, and better accord with Christian humility, to be satisfied with believing the Scriptural assertions, that "God so loved the world, that he gave his only-begotten Son;" that "He who spared not his own Son, but gave him up for us all, — shall he not, with him, freely give us all things?" Is not this enough, without an argument to prove that the *only* way by which a man can be saved is the method of a suffering God?

We will not dwell further on this head, nor examine our friend's argument to show that we cannot consistently, as Unitarians, have any piety. We will try, then, to have it inconsistently.

VI. Great evils to the Church have come from the doctrine of the Trinity.

It has tended to the belief in three Gods. It has tended to a confusion of belief between three Gods of equal power and majesty, united only in counsel; one supreme, and two inferior Deities; one Deity with a threefold manner of manifestation; and a vague, undetermined use of words, with no meaning attached to them; — unhappy confusion, which none have been more ready to recognize and to point out than Trinitarians themselves.

And what shall we say of the continual struggles, conflicts, and bitter controversies, which this doctrine has caused from the time of its entrance into the Church? What is there more disgraceful in the history of the Church, than the mutual persecutions of Arians and Athanasians, and of all the minor sects and parties, engendered by this disputed doctrine?

This is what Dr. Bushnell says of one of these matters; and his testimony is, perhaps, sufficient on this point: —

"No man can assert three persons, — meaning three consciousnesses, wills, and understandings, — and still have any intelligent meaning in his mind, when he asserts that they are yet one person; for, as he now uses the term, the very idea of a person is that of an essential, incommunicable monad, bounded by consciousness, and vitalized by self-active will: which being true, he might as well profess to hold that three units are yet one unit. When he does it, his words will, of necessity, be only substitutes for sense.

"At the same time, there are too many signs of the mental confusion I speak of not to believe that it exists. Thus, if the class I speak of were to hear a discourse insisting on the proper personal Unity of God, it would awaken suspicion in their minds, while a discourse insisting on the existence of three persons would be only a certain proof of Orthodoxy; showing that they profess three persons, meaning what they profess, and one person, really not meaning it.

"Such is the confusion produced by attempting to assert a real and metaphysical Trinity of persons in the Divine Nature. Whether the word is taken at its full import, or diminished away to a mere something called a *distinction*, there is produced only contrariety, confusion, practical negation, not light."

So far Dr. Bushnell. On another point, thus testifies Twesten:—

"There are many, to whom the Biblical and religious basis of the doctrine is exceeding sure and precious, who are dissatisfied with the Church form of the doctrine, and even feel themselves repelled or fettered by it. It is to them more negative than positive; more opposed to errors, than giving any insight into truth. It solves no difficulty; it unseals no new revelation."

Twesten goes on to admit that the Trinity has really hemmed in the free movement of the mind, substituting a dead uniformity for a manifold and various life; and yet Twesten is a very strong and able Trinitarian.

VII. The doctrine of the Trinity is a doctrine of philosophy, and not of faith.

As philosophy, it might be ever so true and important; but when brought forward as religion (as it is by Prof. Huntington), it would become at once pernicious. To offer theology for religion, belief for faith, philosophy born of speculative reflection in place of spiritual insight and pious experience, have always been most deleterious both to religion and to philosophy.

The objects of faith are the Father, the Son, and the Holy Spirit. Through Christ, we have access to the Father, in the Spirit. We see the Father revealed to us in the Son; we feel the power of the Spirit in our hearts. This is religion; but this has nothing to do with the doctrine of the Trinity.

VIII. We can trace the gradual formation of the doctrine in the Christian Church.

The following facts we suppose to be incontrovertible: —

1. Down to the time of the Synod of Nice (A.D. 325) the Son was considered to be subordinate, or inferior to the Father, by the great majority of writers and teachers in the Christian Church, and by the multitude of believers; and no doctrine of Trinity existed in the Church.

2. The *Nicene symbol*, which declared Christ to be 'God from God, Light from Light, true God from true God, of the same substance with the Father," * was di-

---

* See the creed in Hagenbach ("History of Doct.," Vol. I. p. 268): Θεὸν ἐκ. Θεοῦ, φῶς ἐκ φωτὸς, Θεὸν ἀληθινὸν ἐκ Θεοῦ ἀληθινοῦ.

rected against the two Arian positions, — that Christ was created, and that there was a time when he did not exist; but it did not declare his equality with God the Father, nor teach the personality of the Holy Spirit, nor say anything of the Trinity.

3. The councils vacillated to and fro during three hundred years, gradually tending toward the present Church doctrine of the Trinity; thus: —

1. *Synod of Nice* (A. D. 325) opposed the Arian doctrine of the creation of Christ out of nothing, and maintained that his substance was derived from that of God.

2. *Synod of Tyre* (A. D. 335) favored the Arians, and deposed Athanasius.

3. *Council of Antioch* (A. D. 343) opposed the views of the Arians, and also the views of their opponents.

4. *Council of Sardica* (A. D. 344) resulted in a division between the Eastern and Western Churches; the East being semi-Arian, and the West Athanasian, in their view of the nature of Christ.

5. The Western Church tending to Sabellianism (taught by Marcellus and his pupil Photinus), this view was condemned by two councils in the East and West; viz.: —

Second Council of Antioch (A. D. 343).
Council of Milan (A. D. 346).

6. Constantius, an Arian emperor, endeavored to make the Western Churches accept the Arian doctrine; and, at two synods (A. D. 353 and 355, at Arelate and Mediolanum), compelled the bishops to sign the condemnation of Athanasius, deposing those who refused to do so.

7. The Arians, being thus dominant, immediately di-

vided into Arians and semi-Arians, — the distinction being the famous distinction between *o* and *oi*. Both parties denied the *Homoousios;* but the semi-Arians admitted the *Homoiousios.*

8. At the Synod of Ancyra (A. D. 358), the semi-Arian doctrine was adopted, and the Arian rejected. The third Synod of Sirmium (A. D. 358) did the same thing.

9. Down to this time (A. D. 360), nothing was said about the Holy Spirit in its relation to the Trinity. The Emperor Valens, an Arian, persecuted the Athanasians from A. D. 364 to 378. Then Theodosius, an Athanasian emperor, persecuted the Arians. Semi-Arianism, however, continued Orthodox in the East.

10. The Nestorian controversy broke out A. D. 430. The Council of Ephesus (A. D. 431) condemned Nestor. The Nestorians (who were Unitarians) separated entirely from the Church, and became the Church of the Persian Empire.

11. The Monophysite controversy broke out. The Council of Chalcedon (A. D. 451) decided that there were two natures in Christ; and the Monophysites separated, and formed the Coptic Church. Their formula was, that "God was crucified in Christ." The Nestorians were too Unitarian, and the Monophysites too Athanasian. The Church decided (against the Nestorians) that Mary was God's mother, but decided (against the Monophysites) that God was not crucified.

12. *First Lateran Council* was called (in A. D. 640) to settle a new point. It having been decided that there were *two* natures in Christ, it was now thought best by many to yield to the Monophysites, — that there was

only one will in Christ. Hence the Monotheletic controversy, finally settled at the, —

13. Sixth General Council (A. D. 680), when *two* wills in Christ were accepted as the doctrine of the Church.

Thus it appears that it took the Church from A. D. 325 to A. D. 680 to settle the questions concerning the relation of Christ to God. During all this time, opinion vacillated between Arianism on the one hand, and Sabellianism on the other. At the end of this period, the Church had become consolidated, and strong enough to compel submission to its opinions; but the relation of the Holy Spirit to the Trinity remained unsettled for several centuries more; and finally the Eastern Church separated altogether from the Western Church on this point. The whole Greek Church remains, to this day, separated from the Latin Church on a question belonging to this very doctrine of the Trinity. So much, then, for Prof. Huntington's assertion, that the Trinity is a doctrine which can almost literally be said to have been believed "always, everywhere, and by all."

IX. The doctrine of the Trinity is opposed to the real divinity of Christ, and to his real humanity; thus undermining continually the faith of the Church in the divine humanity of Jesus Christ the Lord.

Our final and chief objection to the Trinity is, not that it makes Christ divine, but that it does *not* make him so. It substitutes for the divinity of the Father, the Supreme God, which Unitarians believe to dwell in Christ, a subordinate divinity of God the Son. This is subordinate, because derived; and, because derived, dependent. The Son may be said to be "eternally generated;" but this is only an eternal derivation, and does not alter the dependence, but makes it also to be eternal. The tendency of the Church doctrine of the Trinity is always to a belief, not in the Supreme Divinity dwelling in Christ, but in a derived and secondary divinity.

How is it, for example, with the Nicene doctrine concerning Christ? Prof. Huntington claims Nice as Trinitarian (p. 361).

But what says Prof. Stuart concerning the Nicene doctrine? Listen: —

"The Nicene symbol presents the Father as the Monas, or proper Godhead, in and of himself exclusively; it represents him as the *Fons et Principium* of the Son, and therefore gives him superior power and glory. It does not even assert the claims of the blessed Spirit to Godhead; and therefore leaves room to doubt whether it means to recognize a Trinity, or only a Duality." (Moses Stuart, "Bib. Repos.," 1835. Quoted by Wilson, "Trin. Test.," p. 264.)

And how is it with the ante-Nicene fathers, whom Prof. Huntington also considers to be Trinitarian, else certainly his rule of "always, everywhere, and by all," does not hold? If, for the first three hundred years after Christ, there were no Trinitarians, it cannot be said that the Trinity has "always" been held in the Church. Listen, again, to Prof. Stuart, whose learning no one can question: —

"We find that all the fathers before, at, and after the Council of Nice, who harmonize with the sentiments there avowed, declare the Father only to be the self-existent God." (See the whole paragraph in Wilson, "Trin. Test.," p. 267.)

"To be the author of the proper substance of the Son and Spirit, according to the Patristical creed; or to be the author of the *modus existendi* of the Son and Spirit, according to the modern creed, — both seem to involve *the idea of power and glory in the Father, immeasurably above that of the Son and Spirit.*" (Moses Stuart, "Bib. Repos.," 1835.)

So Coleridge asserts that "both Scripture and the Nicene Creed teach a subordination of the Son to the Father, independent of the incarnation of the Son. . . . . . Christ, speaking of himself as the co-eternal Son, says, 'My Father is greater than I.'" (Wilson, "Trin. Test.," p. 270.)

According to the Trinitarian doctrine, then, we do not find God — the Supreme God, our Heavenly Father — in Christ; but a derived, subordinate, and inferior Deity. Not the one universal Parent do we approach, but some mysterious, derived, inscrutable Deity, less than the Father, and distinct from him. Do we not, then, lose the benefit and blessing of the divinity of Jesus? Can we believe him when he says, "He who has seen me has seen the Father"? No: we do not believe that, if we are Trinitarians; but rather, that, having seen him, we have seen "THE SON;" whom Coleridge declares to be an inferior Deity; over whom, Bishop Pearson, in his "Exposition of the Creed," says, the Father holds "pre-eminence," — the Father being "the Origin, the Cause, the Author, the Root, the Fountain, the Head, of the Son." The doctrine of the Trinity is therefore opposed, as Swedenborg ably contends, to the real divinity of Christ.*

---

* Thus speaks Dr. Bushnell on this head ("God in Christ," p. 139) : —

But it is equally opposed to his real humanity. It constantly drives out of the Church the human element in Christ. Prof. Huntington is astonished at Unitarians not perceiving that the humanity of Christ is as dear to Trinitarians as his Deity; yet it cannot be denied, that the mysterious dogma of Deity has quite overshadowed the simple human life of our dear Lord, so that the Church has failed to see the Son of man. All his highest human traits become unreal in the light of this doctrine of his Deity. He is tempted: but that is unreal; for God cannot be tempted. He prays, "Our Father:" but this also is no real prayer; for he is omnipotent, and can need nothing. He encounters opposition, hatred, contumely, and bears it with sweetest composure: but what of that? since, as God, he looked down from an infinite height upon the puny opposition. He agonizes in the garden; but it is imaginary suffering; how can God feel any real agony like man? Jesus ceases to be example, ceases to be our best beloved companion and brother, and becomes a mysterious personage, inscrutable to our thought, and far removed from our sympathy.

"Besides, it is another source of mental confusion, connected with this view of three metaphysical persons, that, though they are all declared to be infinite and equal, they really are not so. The proper deity of Christ is not held in this view. He is begotten, sent, supported, directed, by the Father, in such a sense as really annihilates his Deity. This has been shown in a truly searching and convincing manner by Schleiermacher, in his historical essay on the Trinity; and, indeed, you will see at a glance, that this view of a metaphysical Trinity of persons breaks down in the very point which is commonly regarded as its excellence, — its assertion of the proper Deity of Christ."

We have gone somewhat fully into this discussion, which the secession of a brother and friend from our ranks has roused. He has called to us, with his familiar and eloquent voice, to follow him in accepting the doctrine of the Trinity. We can see no good reason for doing it. His own example and his evident sincerity are more moving arguments than his reasoning. We ask ourselves, May there not be something for us, too, in that doctrine in which he seems to have found so much good? But then we remember, that, while he has been struggling out of Unitarianism into Trinitarianism, others have been as earnestly and honestly struggling out of Trinitarianism into Unitarianism. Some Protestants turn Catholics, and find peace: some Catholics turn Protestants, and also find peace. We have seen converts from Calvinism to Universalism, from Universalism to Calvinism,— converts from and to a liberal theology,— all equally happy in their new faith. One conversion neutralizes another, as evidence for or against the truth of a system.

And now, in taking leave of our brother and of this discussion, we would reach out our hand to him across the dividing gulf of opinion, and say, "God bless you! We stood near you at your ordination, and sympathized with your emotions then in devoting yourself to the service of God. We have seen the manner of your life,— earnest, true, devoted. We are sad at this parting, but believe that you are not wholly taken from us in heart. A few years, brother, and we shall know all which we now see in a glass darkly. Meantime, let us remember the words of Melancthon: 'Hoc est Christum cognoscere, beneficia ejus cognoscere; non, ut illi aiunt, modos incarnationis.'"

TRINITARIANISM NOT THE DOCTRINE OF THE NEW TESTAMENT.*

By Rev. T. S. KING.

LECTURE I.

"For though there be that are called gods, whether in heaven or in earth, (as there be gods many and lords many,) but to us there is but one God, the Father, of whom are all things, and we in him; and one Lord Jesus Christ, by whom are all things, and we by him. Howbeit there is not in every man that knowledge." — 1 Cor. viii. 5, 6, 7.

I shall ask you to consider with me, in two lectures, the Scriptural evidence for the Church doctrine of the Trinity. It will be accepted, I think, as forcible evidence that I have no strong tendency to disputation about this doctrine in which the general faith of Christendom is moulded, if I say that, during a ministry here of more than eleven years, and an experience of fifteen years as a preacher, I have never written a discourse or lecture, or any portion of one, bearing directly upon it. I have not felt, and do not now feel, a desire to attack, or call in question, the forms in which the majority of Christians cast, or imagine that they cast, their

---

* Two Lectures delivered, partly in Review of Rev. Dr. Huntington's Discourse on the Trinity, in the Hollis Street Church, January 7 and 14, 1860.

faith concerning the constitution of the Infinite Personality.

It is chiefly by the instinct of defence that I am moved to ask attention here on the controverted doctrine. In common with thousands, I have read recently the elaborate discourse by a clergyman long prominent and honored in the Unitarian body, now Preacher to the Cambridge University, in which he sets forth, not merely his belief in that dogma, but his conviction that it supplies the only scheme of faith that will produce a working church, a sound piety, and even a lasting and practical belief in the personality of God. Fresh interest will be excited, of course, in the great subject at issue between Trinitarians and Unitarians, by this transit of an eminent preacher from the minority to the majority; and we shall do nothing more than pay proper respect to the volume in which our faith is cast off and arraigned, as well as to our own system of belief, if we make serious inquiry into the Scriptural supports for the doctrine of the Trinity.

The clergyman of whose book I speak lays great stress on the fact that the Trinity is so generally believed in Christendom, and has been the faith of all centuries. In all ages of the Church, he says, "the strong thinkers" have been, upon this point, "essentially and persistently as one." And he quotes the names of twenty-eight prominent theologians, belonging to different ages, countries, and sects, representative men, who are divided by no differences on this article of belief. Yet, in looking at the list attentively, a very interesting fact appears; no name is quoted earlier than the fourth Christian century. Where are the names of the fathers before the year 300, who were sound upon this dogma? What great teacher or saint, during the first six generations after the Apostles, can be produced, who is in accord with any strict and sound Trinitarian theologian of the modern Protestant Church? The evidence from general belief, from the consent of thinkers in different countries and divisions of the Church, however even then it would fail of being conclusive, would be of immensely greater force if we could find the formulæ of modern times indorsed and published by the teachers *nearest* the *apostolic* age. But what if that evidence begins to grow faint as we ascend beyond the year 300? What if, above that period, no theologian or preacher can be found who has framed a definition of the Trinity which would be called safe by any ordinary council in this country?

Now this is the fact. Of the twenty-eight theologians whom Dr. Huntington quotes, the two most learned ones in the English branch of the Church are Dr. Cudworth and Bishop Bull. Yet Dr. Cudworth affirms that the Christian fathers of the first three centuries plainly taught the subordination of Christ to the Father, and did not believe in any such coequality as would exclude inferiority and dependence. And Bishop Bull, who has written the most able defence ever made by an Englishman of the Trinitarian dogma, though holding the theory of subordination, declares that almost all the Christian "writers before Arius's time (320) seem not to have known anything of the invisibility and immensity of the Son of God; and that they often speak of him in such a manner as if, even in respect of his divine nature, he was finite, visible, and circumscribed in place." * Petavius, too, a Jesuit, proves by a thorough discussion of the subject, that the great Christian writers of the first three centuries believed that the Supreme God brought the Son into existence to employ him as his instrument in the formation of the world. And Petavius accuses them of entertaining thus opinions

---

* I do not mean to say that the earlier fathers of the Church taught the system which usually goes by the name of Unitarianism. It would be unjust and foolish to conceal the fact that their scheme of thought was very different, — almost as distant from Unitarianism as it is from Calvinistic Orthodoxy. Nor can any one deny that after the year 200 there was a steady tendency towards such formulæ as were voted by the Councils of Nicæa and Constantinople. But I do not understand how anybody can read the full collection of the evidence by men hostile to Unitarianism, — by Petavius, Burton, Dorner, Bunsen, — and claim that the Christian writers before the time of Origen held any scheme of the Divine Personality that is in harmony with the popular Trinitarianism of to-day.

Dorner acknowledges that Origen (who died A. D. 254) was the first who tried to solve the contradictions of his predecessors as to the substance and rank of the Son, and to put the doctrine of the Logos in a shape that would harmonize with Trinitarianism. To Origen we owe the dogma of the eternally proceeding generation of the Son from the Father. Yet how far Origen was from holding the Trinitarianism of to-day, may be seen when we quote his declaration that " Prayer, properly speaking, is to be offered to the Father only. We first bring our prayers to the only Son of God, the First-born of the whole creation, the Logos of God, and pray to him, and request him, as a High Priest, to offer up the prayers which reach him, to the God over all, to his God and our God." He declares, also that "the Holy Spirit was made by the Logos, the Logos being older than the Spirit." No wonder that Prof. Burton calls this " an unfortunate passage! " Still further, he states his belief that " the power of the Father is greater than that of the Son and of the Holy Ghost. That of the

unworthy of the dignity of the Son, and altogether absurd. Still another Trinitarian scholar, M. Jurieu, a learned French Calvinist, maintains the position that the teachers of the first three centuries held the inequality of the Son with the Father, and his birth in time, and asserts that the mystery of the Trinity remained without its right form or shape until the Council

---

Son is greater than that of the Holy Ghost; and again the power of the Holy Ghost surpasses that of all other holy things."

We might quote a chain of passages from Clement of Rome, who touches the lifetime of St. Paul, to Lactantius, A. D. 310, to prove that not one of the fathers within these dates was acquainted with the Orthodox Trinitarianism of modern times, which claims to be the faith " once delivered to the saints." But it might, perhaps, be said or thought that we did not fairly represent the faith of those early centuries by the extracts. It may be accounted of more value if we quote the testimony of Bunsen, whose learning will not be questioned, and who will not be suspected of partiality for Unitarian conceptions of Christianity. In the first volume of his great work, " Christianity and Mankind," the history of the Church is rapidly sketched in outlines of the thought of the chief theologians to the close of the seventh generation from the Crucifixion. And he tells us that "the doctrinal system of the Ante-Nicene Church is irreconcilable with the letter and authority of the formularies of the Constantinian and in general of the Byzantine councils, *as much as these are with the Bible and common sense.*" (Preface, p. 19.) The problem of the divine nature, he affirms, was solved "illogically and unhistorically" by the councils of the fourth century. "The latter view having triumphed by a persecuting and often unscrupulous majority, the victorious hierarchical party canonized, in the course of the two next blood-stained centuries, the confession of its intellectual bankruptcy into a confession of faith, and made submission to it the condition of churchmanship and the badge of eternal salvation." (Page 81.) Again, "if one reads all that the old Protestant schools have said on it (the first verse of

of Constantinople, in 381. (See Emlyn's Tracts, Vol. II. pp. 277 *et seq.*)

Now, of what importance is the concurrent belief of the great branches of the Christian Church in a doctrine which begins to fade just as we approach the centuries when the tradition must have been purest, — if it is only after Christianity was "improved and beautified by

---

John's Gospel) during these 250 years, there is scarcely anything, philosophically speaking, but chaff to be found in it. The text ('the word was God') is explained by theological terms and formularies, which at least must be taken to be conventional, till they are shown to be the necessary and only possible deductions from the sacred text. Now this has never been proved; and I have no hesitation in saying that no honest and intelligent criticism can prove them to be sufficiently warranted, Biblically or philosophically, for exclusive acceptance; nor are they strictly reconcilable with the true, genuine, uninterpolated writings of the fathers of the first, second, and third centuries. I speak advisedly; for I have read these writings with a sincere desire to understand and appreciate them; and in judging them I use nothing but the liberty, or rather I exercise the duty, of a Protestant Christian, searching for truth." (Page 408.) Once more: "The theological system built up since (the time of Origen) is conventional; it is based upon misinterpretation and upon council formularies, which were a wall between the theologian and Scripture as well as reason. These formularies of the fourth, fifth, sixth, and seventh centuries are the confession of a failure, and have made the most sublime part of our theology conventional and hollow." (Page 307.)

Professor Huntington is as unfortunate, also, in claiming a persistent unity among those who have defended the Trinity since the fourth century, as in appealing to the universal voice of the Church in its behalf. There are, and have always been, differences as marked between defenders of the Trinity in their conceptions of that dogma, as any that separate Trinitarians from Unitarians.

synods and councils" that the chorus commences? The fact is, the only creed known to the first three centuries was this: "I believe in One God, the Father Almighty, maker of heaven and earth; and in Jesus Christ, his only Son our Lord, who was conceived by the Holy Ghost, born of the Virgin Mary, suffered under Pontius Pilate, was crucified, dead and buried: he descended into hell; the third day he rose again from the dead; he ascended into heaven, and sitteth on the right hand of God, the Father Almighty; from thence he shall come to judge the quick and the dead. I believe in the Holy Ghost; the Holy Catholic Church; the communion of saints; the forgiveness of sins; the resurrection of the body; and the life everlasting. Amen." Not a word here of the Triune Deity, of the constitution of the Divine Personality, of coequal constituents in the Infinite Oneness; not a word of any feature of that clear Trinitarian scheme of thought, with its adjuncts and corollaries, in which alone Dr. Huntington sees "the sublime working-scheme of revelation and redemption," and which he says has been so widely believed, that it is "irreverent towards Providence" to suppose that it is "unfounded in revelation and truth."

All this, of course, is of trifling consequence, compared with the testimony of the New Testament. Here the question must be brought for settlement, whatever the teaching of the Church up to the year 100 may be. But it is right to sift all sweeping statements about the unanimous voice of the Church in favor of modern Trinitarianism; for they are not true. The last fifteen hundred years are of immeasurably less consequence than the first three hundred. And it was not until the year

325 that a creed was formed, affirming the eternity of Christ; while no creed establishing the proper Deity of the Holy Ghost was voted until A. D. 381. There were most strenuous and bitter struggles and contests against these dogmas. And yet neither of these creeds contains any such statement as that the Father and the Son, or the Father, Son, and Holy Ghost, constitute numerically but one God. This declaration was reserved for a still later period, during the settling shadows of the Middle Age.

Let us come then to the testimony of the New Testament. Do the documents that constitute the New Testament reveal a Trinity of coequal persons, emerging from the ineffable and veiled Godhead, so that we can know of no Deity independent of that threefold distinction? This is the doctrine which is emphatically stated to us in the volume to which I have already alluded, as the basis of the Christian religion and revelation. Now let us take notice that the question is not concerning the mystical nature, or even the Divinity, of Christ. The question is not whether the New Testament reveals the pre-existence, the miraculous birth, the superhuman and even superangelic rank of Jesus; nor whether it declares to us that the Divine quickening and grace have been poured into humanity through a nature interpenetrated and transfused with the Divine essence, so that he was the image of God, and poured out the Spirit of God upon the world.

We allow points to be confused, too often, in conducting this inquiry, which ought rigidly to be kept separate. Proofs are often passed to the credit of the

Trinitarian formulæ, which weigh only in behalf of the super-earthly origin and rank of Jesus. I freely admit that no one can fairly read some of the books of the New Testament, and deny that they teach the supremacy of Christ in the hierarchy of created natures, and the dependence of the world upon his voluntary assumption of human nature for its spiritual life. But the passages that establish this view are not pertinent, let us remember, as proof of the Trinitarian doctrine. It is a very delicate and very difficult matter to shape a statement of the origin, rank, and work of Christ which shall harmonize all that the New Testament books present to us concerning his pre-existence, his birth, his relation to the Infinite Spirit when here, his exaltation, and his position in the conscious universe throughout eternity.

If ordinary Unitarianism has not fairly interpreted and fully reproduced the predominant Scriptural doctrine on this point, let it be impeached by any sect or theologian who is willing to stand by those documents, disconnected from any other creed, and without additions from Church history. But let us see to it that lines of evidence are not crossed, and that proofs are not carried over to one doctrine which can be rightfully summoned only for another.

The simple point is this: Does the New Testament clearly reveal the Tri-personality or Threeness of the Godhead, so that, as Christians, our idea of the Unity of God must be composed of three constituents? and do Christ and the Holy Ghost, coequal in dignity, personality, eternity, and infinity, form two of those constituents? Is this conception of the Godhead the core of the Christian faith, as we gather it from the New Testament, so that we may call it "the sublime working-scheme of Revelation"?

If it is, of course one thing is certain: we shall find it distinctly asserted, in the pages that bear the first impress of the organic thought of the Church. It should be in their warp. Revelation, certainly, will not attempt to work independent of its "working-scheme."

And let us look first at the three earliest Gospels, — Matthew, Mark, and Luke. In all the teaching of Christ throughout their pages, do we find any declaration of a threefoldness in the Divine personality or essence? Not a word. The Jews were Unitarians. They needed the disclosure of the Trinity in positive and explicit speech, if they were to be drawn at all to belief in it; and yet, throughout all the conversations of Jesus up to the Crucifixion, as recorded in the first three Evangelists, no hint is given of any doctrine other than the old Hebrew faith in the absolute oneness of the First Cause. The Trinitarian formula is not mentioned. The highest doctrine which Christ announces is his Sonship, — that he is the Anointed, the Son of the living God. Now, whatever this means, it is never for a moment connected with any claim of equality with the Father, or any recognition of other than constant spiritual dependence; nay, it is not even connected with any statement of his pre-existence.

Not only does Jesus, in these biographies, affirm and imply by his teaching and his whole spiritual attitude the doctrine of the Unity of God as the Jews had always conceived it; not only does he declare that "there is none good but one, that is God," and give a model of prayer, which recognizes no second object, or even medium of worship; not only does he conceal from his disciples the mystery of a union of two natures in his own personality, and struggle and pray in Gethsemane, as though he needed strength from the Father, and not from an equal Deity veiled within his own form; but he expressly declares that his knowledge is limited. "Of that day and that hour knoweth no man; no, not the angels which are in heaven; neither the Son, but the Father." One would think that it would be difficult to bring such a passage into fellowship with the requirements of the Trinitarian definition. Dr. Huntington puts it to an entirely original use. He tells us: "For him who has all power in heaven and earth to say, 'Of that day and hour knoweth not the Son,' is condescension indeed! It brings God near as in his unabated attributes he could not be brought." "*Condescension!*" But is it *true*? Must not the Son, who is "rooted forever in the Godhead," be omniscient? And if so, could Christ honestly say that the Son, whom he discriminates from man, and from angels, is ignorant of a date in the future spiritual history of man?

This strange silence of the first three Evangelists as to Christ's Deity, or a Trinity, did not fail to attract the notice of the earliest Church fathers after the doctrine of the Trinity was established. Chrysostom, the eloquent preacher of the year 400, did not hesitate to say that Matthew, Mark, and Luke did not comprehend the depth of the Gospel. They were "like little children, who hear, but do not understand what they hear, being occupied with cakes and childish playthings." It was John, he said, who taught "what the angels themselves did not know before he declared it." The doctrine of the proper divinity of Christ, he maintained, was not published at first, "because the world was not advanced to it. Matthew, Mark, and Luke did not state what was suitable to Christ's dignity, but what was fitting for their hearers." And several of the other fathers declared that the proper divinity of Christ was thus concealed through his personal ministry, in order to elude the vigilance and hostility of Satan. They generally maintained that it was John to whom was committed the unfolding of the Deity of Jesus.

And to-day the principal quotations against Unitarianism drawn from the Gospels are selected from that of John. Yet where is there a statement of the Trinity — that there are three coequal persons in the Godhead — to be found in it? Is it in the first chapter, among those vast vague verses, that tell us "in the beginning was the word, and the word was with God, and the word was God?" But the Holy Spirit is not mentioned there. Those verses, if they are obscure as to their positive philosophical contents, are plain enough as to what they exclude. And if they were written to unfold or suggest to us the mystery of the Divine nature, the Trinity must be dropped as an Evangelical doctrine, for the third personality is not even hinted.

But we shall be referred, perhaps, to the conversation in the 14th, 15th, and 16th chapters, where Jesus promises his disciples to send the Comforter, the Spirit of Truth, by which their minds shall be enlightened, and he shall be glorified, after his crucifixion. But is there any allusion in those chapters to the Comforter as a portion of a threefold Divine Essence, of which Jesus himself was another portion?

Nay, grant that a separate personality and divine rank must be ascribed to the Comforter, are we not forbidden to imagine that an infinite Tripersonality is to be discerned in those chapters, by the very terms in which the office of the Comforter is outlined? "He shall not speak of himself; but whatsoever he shall hear, that shall he speak; . . . . . he shall receive of mine, and shall shew it unto you." Is this a revelation of a person coequal with the Father in the Godhead? Perhaps Dr. Huntington will listen more attentively to a voice urging this argument from the ancient Church. Novatian, an ante-Nicene father, quotes this same passage, and says: "If he received of Christ the things which he declared, Christ is then greater than the Comforter; for he would not receive from Christ, unless he were less than Christ." In another passage of this discourse, Dr. Huntington, speaking of the Holy Spirit, says: "If he is personal, no considerable number of men have ever been found to question that he is God, nor to hesitate at the Tri-unity." We cannot understand the logic, even if the fact of the separate personality be demonstrated. Indeed, the writer above quoted, and the "considerable number of men," in the first six generations after the Apostles, who believed in the separate personality of the Spirit, never heard of such an hypothesis as Tri-unity.

Moreover, if the four chapters in John, of which we are speaking, reveal that doctrine, it was the *first time* that Jesus had unfolded it to his personal followers. It must, therefore, have stood out pre-eminent over all other addresses and interviews in their minds and memory. Is it not strange, therefore, if that was the truth they derived from it, that none of the other Evangelists has reported it, or any fragment from it? Surely, whatever else they might have left unrecorded, they would not have omitted *that*, — surely it would not have been left to a single reporter of the conversation of Jesus to save the basis doctrine, the very " working-scheme " of revelation for the world.

The Gospel of John abounds, equally with the others, in expressions of the dependence and inferiority of Christ. The strongest language in it, used by Jesus himself, which is in harmony, at any point, with the Trinitarian doctrine, is in the verses, " He that hath seen me hath seen the Father," and " I and my Father are one." Yet if the other equally strong language, " My Father is greater than I," " The Son can do nothing of himself," " As the Father hath life in himself, so hath he given to the Son to have life in himself," were not sufficient to check the Trinitarian inference, another passage is conclusive, by showing in what sense Jesus used that mystic form of speech. He prays for all that believe on him, " that they all may be one; as thou, Father, art in me, and I in thee, that they also may be one in us: . . . . . *I in them*, and thou in me, that they may be made perfect in one." Is not this just as strong an argument for the lifting of *believers* into participation in the Godhead, as the other verse is for lifting Christ to that awful height?

Let me say, however, that I do not believe the Gospel of John teaches the mere humanity of Christ. I admit that many Unitarian interpreters have put a forced construction upon much of its affirmation, to make it accord with the lowest form of Unitarian belief. To me it declares plainly the pre-existence of Christ as a super-mortal nature, dearly beloved of God, made of the Divine substance, who came to declare God and reflect him, as it were, in a darkened world, and to infuse the divine spirit and love by a life of obedience and sacrifice in the world, as the organic centre of a sanctified society on earth.

But how different is this from the Trinitarian doctrine, which is never stated in the whole of John's Gospel, or even from the conception of the proper Deity of Christ. Dr. Huntington tells us, in one of the most surprising statements of his volume, that if we believe on the authority of John's Gospel that Christ "came forth" from the Father, "came down," "left the glory he had with the Father before the world was," acknowledging thus a personal pre-existence, we must see that the passages "establish a proper Divinity." (He means Deity.) He tells us that there is no middle ground. It is just this kind of hasty and indiscriminate assertion that has been the bane and disgrace of Scriptural interpretation. Instead of striving by patient and exhaustive study of the facts of a book to see what its theory really is, theologians have often narrowed a controversy, or an interpretation, to one of two hypotheses, not stopping to conjecture whether, by refraining from hypotheses and looking steadily at the facts, the Biblical doctrine might not turn out different from any of the moulds of their fancy or pre-judgment. I do not believe that there is a single sect which to-day reproduces fairly the prominent points of the apostolic theology, and the conception of St. John's Gospel, or that even thoroughly understands it, — and simply for the reason that interpretation begins with one of two theories in view, theories which have grown up since the apostolic time, and were not dreamed of then. Any man who wishes to restore in his own faith or preaching the scheme of Christology in St. John's Gospel, must abandon the Trinitarian conception, and the equal deity of God the Son; drop all such notions as that Christ must be God if he is not merely man; and gain a view of him as the imparting agent of the Divine life from God to man, and to that end leaving a native glory and joy, in which he was the dearest but dependent object of Infinite affection. That Gospel is equally opposed to the humanitarian and Trinitarian theory.

But before we pass from the testimony offered by the four biographies, we must not overlook the passage at the close of Matthew, which is regarded as a very strong support, if not the corner-stone, of the New Testament evidence of the Trinity. I mean the command of Jesus: "Go ye, therefore, and teach all nations, baptizing them in the name of the Father, and of the Son, and of the Holy Ghost." Dr. Huntington lays great stress on this passage. It is the text of his discourse. Jesus uttered it just as he was passing from the world, to his Apostles, and in it he gave the substance and sum of his religion. "That central and sublime verity," we are told, "on which the whole matter of the Gospel rested, was to be condensed into a brief, comprehensive, significant sentence." "Our faith is summoned to the three persons of the one God." "There is nothing in the situation, the relation, or the contents of the Divine formula, to suggest that either of the three is less than the others, or less than God."

But now read that formula in the light of these statements. Does it state that such is the constitution of the Godhead? Does it say that these are three personalities, included in or issuing from the Infinite substance, making it three to human thought, and yet only one numerically and in essence? It says nothing of the kind. It does not imply or hint any doctrine of the absolute personality. It does not commission the Apostles to baptize, as Dr. Huntington asserts, "in the Triune name." It offers a formula which suggests the great forces of the Christian religion, the Fatherhood of God, the Sonship of Christ, the gift of the Holy Spirit, and is silent as to explanations. Will any Trinitarian scholar say, that, hearing those words uttered for the first time, he could attribute no other meaning to them than a declaration of the mysterious threefoldness or tripersonality of one God? They may mean any one of a score of conceptions, and what particular meaning they bear must be determined, the first time we hear them, by the general system of thought of the person from whom they are published.

Now this is *the first time* that such a formula appears in the teaching of Christ. It is the *only* time it occurs in the whole New Testament; and are we to fasten at once upon a significance developed four hundred years afterwards, and say *that* is the only sense it can possibly bear? It has been asserted that this must represent the Godhead, because baptism would not be offered in any other name than the Highest. But the Jews were baptized into Moses, and the Samaritans were baptized into Mount Gerizim. Some have asked this question: Would Christ, if he is not God,— if he is only a man, — have associated himself with God in such a solemn phrase and symbol? But suppose that he is far more than man, though entirely subordinate to God, and is the channel through which the Infinite character and grace are published on the earth. *Then* is it surprising that his name should be interwoven with the paternal name and the quickening spirit in a formula of baptism into his religion and Church? Paul says, "I charge thee before God, and the Lord Jesus Christ, *and the elect angels*, that thou observe these things!" Here created natures are put in fellowship with the Almighty in a religious statement. The Apostles say in one of their letters missive, in the Book of Acts, "It seemed good to the Holy Ghost, *and to us*." What do we say to this intertwining of Divine and mortal judgment in one phrase? Paul says, "In the name of the Lord Jesus Christ, when ye are gathered together, *and my spirit*." Did he make himself equal to Christ? The salutation in the book of Revelation is, "Grace be unto you, and peace, from Him which is, and which was, and which is to come; *and from the seven spirits which are before his throne;* and from Jesus Christ." Are the seven spirits part of the Infinite Personality?

It has been a favorite position with those who have gone deeply into the argument for the support of the Trinity, that Christ reserved the doctrine during his earlier ministry. His hearers and his intimate disciples, it has been said, could not have borne the splendor and the terror of the truth that the Incarnate God, the second member of the Infinite Three, was in familiar converse with them, instructing their ignorance, healing their sick, reclining at their tables, taking their little children in his arms. In order to give his religion the opportunity to mingle itself naturally with the feeling and thought of Palestine, Christ, it is affirmed, was obliged to veil his glory till the close of his earthly manifestation, and therefore it is, we are told, that throughout the bulk of Matthew, Mark, and Luke, so little appears that seems to be in harmony with the proper Deity of Christ, or with the Trinity.

If this is so, of course the revelation will be the more potent and dazzling, when it is made. The contrast will be the greater on account of the former darkness; and we shall surely find *all* the Evangelists in agreement as to the time and form of the stupendous announcement, — the falling of the veil that had screened the Infinite from their gaze. We shall find unmistakable traces in the sacred books of the date and method of that disclosure.

Some have supposed that Jesus made it at the Last Supper, on the institution of the communion rite, in the conversation about the Comforter and the prayer that followed, as related in the 14th, 15th, 16th, and 17th chapters of John. But strangely not a word of that discourse or prayer is narrated by either of the other biographers in their accounts of the Supper. We can explain this discrepance and omission on no other theory than the Trinitarian hypothesis just stated. If the disclosure of the Deity of Jesus and the Triune constitution of the Infinite was first clearly made at that time, is it possible, I ask you, that it should have been overlooked by the three Evangelists who *first* wrote the account of

Jesus's ministry,—and that it should have been reserved for John to recall it, who did not prepare his Gospel, according to the admission of Trinitarian scholars, until a generation later? Can *any* satisfactory answer be made to this objection? It seems to me to shut out the possibility of explanation.

Others maintain that it was after the resurrection, and just before the ascension, that Christ unfolded the mystery of his person and of the Godhead. The announcement was made in the formula of the great commission,—"Go and teach all nations, baptizing them in the name of the Father, and of the Son, and of the Holy Ghost." Still we should expect to find *all* the Evangelists agreeing in the disclosure of the mystery. We should expect to find it the focal point of light and power on their pages. But we are struck again with the fact that only Matthew records this formula as having been used by Jesus. Neither Mark, Luke, nor John alludes to the utterance of any such phrase by Christ at the close of his career, or any statement concerning his own Deity or the threefoldness of God. If, as Dr. Huntington tells us, "in every respect, it was the natural and fitting time for the decisive, explicit communication of the one essential characteristic truth of his religion;" if now "we listen with breathless anxiety to hear what Christianity means;" feeling that "now, if ever, Christ will distinctly proclaim the doctrine of Christendom;" and especially if this doctrine, so solemnly uttered, be the Trinity, which has *never before* been stated by Jesus to his disciples, is it possible that it should have been omitted by Luke and John, as carelessly as if no such conversation had taken place? Is it possible that

Mark should have recorded the general command of Christ to teach and baptize, but have left, as he did, the Trinitarian formula out of his record? Do not these facts prove as clearly as moral demonstration can be made out, that the baptismal command did not represent to the Apostles the doctrine of the Trinity, for the first time clearly stated by Jesus to his followers?

And yet the strength of the case is not exhausted yet. If the phrases of the great commission, at the close of Matthew's Gospel, was the comprehensive statement of the Trinity into which believers were to be baptized, — if it was the new and clear revelation of Jesus, at the conclusion of his ministry, of a mystery concealed wholly or in part from his disciples until then, — we shall surely see the effect of it in the first preaching of the Apostles, after Jesus passes from the world. The Book of the Acts will be one continual and blazing commentary upon that revelation, last made to the Apostles, of the Deity of Christ and the Trinity of the Godhead. If the first three Gospels are obscure, that book will be luminous, and will crush any possibility of Unitarianism in the Church. Some Trinitarian scholars, indeed, have maintained that it was not till after Christ's ascension, till the day of Pentecost, when the Spirit was given to the Apostles, that they were fully enlightened as to the great mystery of the Godhead.

But now what shall we say when all the speeches of the Apostles in Jerusalem, just after Pentecost, contain no statement of the Deity of Jesus, and no allusion to a threefold personality, or any mystery in the constitution of the Godhead? And these were sermons preached to *Unitarian Jews*. Read those opening chapters of the Acts, and see how the burden of the speeches is the resurrection of Jesus, " a man approved of God among you by miracles, and wonders, and signs, which God did by him in the midst of you," by the power of God, and his exaltation by the Almighty to be the Prince and Saviour of men. Would it have been possible for Peter and Stephen, with the truth just revealed to their minds of the Deity of Jesus and his equality with the Father, to make the addresses recorded in the first half of the Book of Acts, — addresses from which hundreds must derive their first impressions of Christ's rank, — which not only do not state the doctrine, but from which it could not be inferred, and whose theology would not be considered sound and evangelical, if made by a young Orthodox candidate before the mildest Orthodox council of New England?

But follow every Apostle in his ministry through the pages of the Book of Acts. In no sermon or speech of any speaker, in any missionary tour, is the Deity of Christ stated. Jesus has been raised from the dead; Jesus is the Christ; Jesus has been appointed judge of the world, and is to return to rule over Christendom; the Divine Spirit is given as the result and seal of faith in Christ's Messiahship; — I ask you to read the Book of the Acts through continuously, and see if these are not the exhaustive ideas of the Apostles in their first preaching of Christ to the world. We are told that the baptismal phrase was given by Christ to the Apostles, at the close of his ministry, as a statement of the Trinity, and the creed into which converts must be baptized. Yet not a single instance is recorded in all Peter's and Paul's tours of the use of that formula in baptism. That ordinance was always administered in the name of Christ alone. The phrase "Father, Son, and Holy Ghost" does not occur in the whole record of the early missionary preaching of the first teachers of the Church. And if that Book of Acts should be taken out of the New Testament, and handed over as a dictionary to a theological professor in Princeton or Andover, the Trinitarian creed of either of those institutions could not be drawn from it by any recombination of its verses.

It has often been said that Paul's speech on Mars Hill, the first publication of the Gospel in the most cultured city of Europe, is entirely Unitarian. It is so unevangelical that it could not to-day be accepted as a Tract, to be issued by the Tract Society, as a statement of Christianity, any more than the Sermon on the Mount could. It has not in it any of what are called the distinguishing doctrines of grace. And all the speeches are equally destitute of the Trinitarian doctrine. It is doubtful even if the pre-existence of Jesus, his superiority in rank to a great prophet supernaturally raised from the dead, and made the Spiritual Priest and Ruler of the race by the Almighty, could be gathered from that whole book. However this may be, the doctrine of the oneness and simplicity of God, as the Jews had always understood it, is not disturbed by any allusion.

The only reference, in the sermon of Dr. Huntington, to the Book of Acts, is his quotation of this passage from one of the addresses recorded in it: "The

God of our fathers raised up Jesus; him hath God exalted to be a Prince and a Saviour, for to give repentance to Israel and forgiveness of sins." On this passage Dr. Huntington makes this comment: "Is it not right to *ask* him who gives repentance and forgiveness of sins, to do it?" Grant it; but does the asking of spiritual help from a glorified nature whom "God hath exalted," prove that being a mysterious, indefinable part of a threefold God? Suppose that the Apostles thought it right to pay spiritual honor to the risen Jesus, does that prove him to have been in their conception the uncreated Deity? They certainly believed him to be the Son of God in a very exalted and peculiar sense; but the question before us is, Did they believe him to be *God the Son*? And further, did they believe him to be one of a Triune Infinite, each equal to the other, each possessing a separate consciousness, and all forming but one Substance and Will? Until evidence and passages are brought to establish this point, the needs of the Trinitarian position are not met.

And on this point, we repeat, the Book of Acts is not only silent, but opposed. It must be accounted opposed, if it is simply silent. For, according to the Trinitarian hypothesis, here is the great mystery announced by the ascending Christ as he has closed his ministry of humiliation, that he has been God veiled in the flesh, and that the Father and the Holy Spirit are coequal with him in a union which makes only one being; and the Apostles, educated rigid Unitarians, who receive it, and who go out to preach the new Gospel, never state it in Jerusalem, in Samaria, in Joppa, in Antioch, in Macedonia, in Athens, in Ephesus, in Rome! In a dozen years of earnest preaching by various men, it does not appear. No record of any baptism into the threefold name is given. They speak always of Jesus commissioned and exalted by the Almighty, after his death, to be the head of a Universal Church. And there is no account in any act of worship, of any prayer or hymn commencing or closing with adoration to Father, Son, and Holy Ghost. Could this be true of any missionaries now going to various countries to preach the Gospel for the first time? Would the salaries of any six or twelve men, of whom such reports came from Burmah or the Sandwich Islands to the American Board, be continued to them another quarter?

I have been thus particular with this document, because we generally conduct the discussion about the Trinity or the Atonement too loosely, by quoting texts from different books, some bearing on one point and some on another, bringing them together as a worker in mosaic makes a bird, or a figure, or a temple, out of various kinds and bits and colors of stone. This would be a tolerable method, perhaps, if the New Testament was one book, written in chapters by one man, continuously, and with one object steadily in view. Then the defect of evidence in one chapter might be compensated by fulness in another. But each book is a separate production. And the Book of Acts, following directly after the first three Gospels, in date far earlier than the Gospel of John, is the record of the first preaching of Christianity for a dozen years, by personal disciples of Christ, and by Paul, in their earliest enthusiasm, when its characteristic doctrines must be brought out clearly to hearers in different countries, who listen to it for the first time. And if the doctrine of the Trinity is not there; if the Deity of Christ is not stated in any of its pages; if no ascription of praise to Father, Son, and Spirit goes up from any of its chapters, — I confess that I know not how a more fatal blow can be dealt upon the assertion that it forms part of original Christianity. If I were to become a Trinitarian, it could be only on the Catholic ground that tradition is superior to Scripture, and that the Holy Spirit from time to time enlightens councils and popes to bring out and clear up doctrines that were concealed, or not amply stated, by the earliest promulgators of the word.

In the lecture next Sunday afternoon, I shall ask you to consider the teaching of Paul on the same doctrine. And I wish that you might all, during the week, as I have during the last week, read the whole New Testament through carefully, to see what is its teaching on the point, Is God three, or is he one? Is Christ subordinate to him in heaven now, as once on earth, or is he coequal in power, majesty, and underived life? Study it reverently, study it faithfully, study it in unbroken charity to all that hold, or that pass to, a different view.

And that we may not close to-day with a controversial temper, let us consider, in the language of one who has written one of the most powerful discourses against the Trinity in English literature, — James Martineau of England, — the value of Christ to a Unitarian, even if he holds the humanitarian scheme: " Him we accept, not indeed as very God, but as the true image of God, commissioned to show what no written doctrinal record could declare, — the entire moral perfections of Deity. The universe gives us the scale of God, and Christ his Spirit. We climb to the infinitude of his nature by the awful pathway of the stars, where whole forests of worlds quiver here and there, like a small leaf of light. The scope of his intellect and the majesty of his rule are seen in the tranquil order and everlasting silence that reign through the fields of his volition. And the Spirit that animates the whole is like that of the Prophet of Nazareth; the thoughts that fly upon the swift light throughout creation, charged with fates unnumbered, are like the healing mercies of one that passed no sorrow by. A faith that spreads around and within the mind a Deity thus sublime and holy, feeds the light of every pure affection, and presses with omnipotent power on the conscience; and our only prayer is that we may walk as children of such light."

LECTURE II.

"There is one body and one spirit, even as ye are called in one hope of your calling; one Lord, one faith, one baptism; one God and Father of all, who is above all, and through all, and in you all." — Ephesians iv. 4, 5, 6.

In the lecture of last Sunday afternoon, we treated the evidence bearing on the doctrine of the Trinity, which is yielded by a careful examination of the four Gospels and the Book of Acts. To-day our chief object is to pass in review, for the same purpose, the Epistles of St. Paul.

We are considering the doctrine of the Trinity especially in relation to the recent assertion of it in a remarkable discourse, by the preacher to the Cambridge University. This is his condensed statement of the doctrine, as he holds it, having abandoned for it the Unitarianism which he once preached, but which he now impeaches as at war with Scripture, and incompetent to nurture a sound piety and a working church. "In the transcendent, removed, and awful depth of his Absolute Infinitude, which no understanding can pierce, the Everlasting and Almighty God lives in an existence of which our only possible knowledge is gained by lights thrown back from revelation. Out of that ineffable and veiled Godhead, — the groundwork, if we may say so, of all Divine manifestation, or theophany, —

there emerge to us in revelation the three whom we rightly call persons, — Father, Son, and Holy Ghost, — with their several individual offices, mutual relations, operations towards men, and perfect unity together.* Holding fast the prime and positive fact of this unity, we have given us, as an equal maker of faith, the Threeness. We know of no priority to that Threeness; of no epoch when it was not; of no Deity independent of that threefold distinction. A question at that point takes us over into realms utterly inscrutable to thought. We conceive of God always, not as

---

* Dr. Huntington's theory of the Trinity, carefully scrutinized, displays a singular inconsistency with itself, as well as with the Scripture he adduces in its support. He makes Father, Son, and Spirit equally manifestations of the obscure abyss of the Godhead. He tells us that " the qualities of the unutterable deific substance are present in each." " The eternal Son," he says, " is seen remaining rooted for ever in the Godhead, having the basis of his being unchanged, deific, uncreated." " Christ comes forth out of the Godhead as the Son, the Saviour." Of course, then, the peculiarity of his scheme is that " the Father " is no less a form of manifesting the unspeakable Deity than the Son. They "emerge" equally as theophanies. And yet he tells us, in the same paragraph, that the Son is eternally begotten of the Father, — a theophany from a theophany, — contradicting thus the statement that he issues, equally with the Father and Spirit, from the infinite substance which is their common base, the " God in whom they are all one," from whom " these three personalities issue forth to take up their merciful and glorious offices."

Dr. Huntington seems to have been conscious of this ill-adjustment of parts in his scheme. For he tells us on the 371st page, that by " thinking patiently " we shall see that " human language could not so well represent these infinite realities as by using the same term, 'Father,' sometimes for the Absolute Godhead, and sometimes for that relative paternal person in the Godhead brought

Absolute Being, but as in relations, in process, in act. And in such relations, process, act, we behold him only as Three : — the Son eternally begotten of the Father, not subordinate in nature or essence, nor created, nor beginning, but consubstantial with the Father : — the Holy Ghost ever proceeding from the Father and the Son, not in time, nor made out of nothing, but one in power, and glory, and eternity with them both."

This doctrine, which Dr. Huntington calls the working scheme of Revelation, we have sought in the four Gospels and the Book of Acts, written by Jews who were educated in the strictest Unitarianism, and published

---

to view only when the Son and the Spirit appear." But after "thinking patiently," we cannot imagine why the New Testament could not state Professor Huntington's theory as clearly as he has done it. We cannot conceive how human language can so well represent any utterable realities as by consistently stating them. If the Son, as Dr. Huntington clearly enough states, is a direct emanation, like the Father, from the Godhead, we do not see why the New Testament should use the word "Father" for the Absolute God, speak of the Son as issuing from him, and thus confuse the whole subject.

But if the New Testament, as is the fact, does not say anything at all about Father, Son, and Spirit emerging as three personalities from one deific substance, we cannot conjecture where Dr. Huntington found *the material* for his theory, especially his authority for calling it "the working scheme of revelation and redemption." We may be told that the whole subject is such a mystery that language and reasoning are not competent to contain or outline it. Why, then, make a theory about it? Why not leave the whole matter where Scripture leaves it, with no Triune statement or suggestion? If a theologian offers a theory of the mystery, we expect that to be self-consistent through the compass of one paragraph : he cannot protect *that* from scrutiny by the plea of mystery.

first — with the exception of John's Gospel — in Unitarian Palestine. We have not found any such doctrine there. We have found passages that imply a very high and mysterious rank for Jesus Christ; but we have not found any language in which this confession of the Cambridge preacher can possibly be stated. All the Scriptural phrases from those books which he could quote to sustain such a position, would not even suggest his doctrine to one that had never heard of it, let them be put together as cunningly as the most partisan Trinitarian theologian could arrange them; while the positive and repeated expressions of those books, and their drift, are at war with such a Triune definition of the Godhead.

We are now to seek the testimony of the Pauline epistles upon the same point. But before such an inquiry, let us glance at the books of the New Testament which remain after those epistles, the four Gospels, and the Acts are examined.

Study the general letter of James to the Jewish Christians. Ask yourself if the doctrine of the Trinity which I have just quoted could be derived from that? The Holy Spirit is not mentioned in it. The Deity of Christ is not stated or implied. Yet it deals with the questions of prayer, justification, the tests of discipleship, and the reception of spiritual blessings from heaven. It would not be possible for an Orthodox clergyman to treat the themes which the Epistle of James unfolds, without using the characteristic phrases of the Trinitarian dogma. He would be suspected of heresy, or his discourse would be pronounced unsavory, if he did not. Yet James wrote his epistle to men who had been trained as Unitarians, and who would have needed to be confirmed by apostolical authority in a Trinitarian faith. A very distinguished living scholar, not a Unitarian, says of this epistle and the writer of it, "Real justice and practical charity to the brethren, true humility and thankfulness to God, no longer under the servitude of ordinances, but under the perfect law of liberty; these were in his eyes the substance of the message which Christ brought to man from God."

Look next at the Epistles of Peter. There is no statement in their chapters of three persons in one God. There is no ascription of praise to the Holy Ghost. In two or three passages the Spirit, or the Holy Spirit, is spoken of, but in ways inconsistent with a belief that it is a separate Divine personality, much less a coequal person in an Eternal Three. And so far is Jesus from receiving in these epistles the title or rank of Deity, he is declared to have been raised from the dead by the superior power of God, to be "on the right hand of God; angels and authorities and powers being made subject unto him." Who made them subject unto him, if by nature he is "one in power, and glory, and eternity with the Father"?

The Epistle of Jude has no Triune statement, distinguishes the Lord Jesus Christ from God, and closes with an offering of praise, not as a Trinitarian epistle would, to Father, Son, and Holy Ghost, but "to the only wise God, our Saviour."

The letter to the Hebrews, which is considered very strong in support of the Atonement, but which was not, probably, written by Paul, or any Apostle, cannot be quoted to originate any Trinitarian hypothesis concerning the Godhead. It not only contains no offering of praise to the Holy Ghost at the close, where God is invoked, but it distinctly denies the coequal rank of Christ with God, while it affirms his super-earthly nature. It begins by saying that God hath in these last days spoken unto us by his Son, whom he hath appointed heir of all things, by whom also he made the worlds. The Son is the brightness of the Father's glory, and the express image of his person, "*being made* so much better than the angels, as he hath by inheritance obtained a more excellent name than they." "Therefore God, even thy God, hath anointed thee with the oil of gladness *above thy fellows.*" "When he bringeth in the first-begotten into the world, he saith, And let all the angels of God worship him." I will not quote other verses from the epistle that affirm decisively the fact that Jesus obtained a higher honor by his earthly suffering and love than he wore before. I need only quote these passages that declare the *native* dignity and splendor of his rank, to show that Trinitarianism is opposed by the Epistle to the Hebrews. For, imagine it said of a coequal member of the Trinity (before the incarnation, so that we cannot say the language is used of his mortal nature), that he is anointed with the oil of gladness above his fellows, and has obtained by inheritance a more excellent name than the angels!

The Epistles of John are often appealed to in proof of the dépendence of the world upon Jesus for its spiritual life, and of the intimate, mystical union of Christ as the Son with the Infinite Father. And there is one verse in the fourth chapter of the First Epistle which declares that "there are three that bear record in heaven, the Father, the Word, and the Holy Ghost; and these three are one." This is the only Trinitarian verse in the New Testament, — the only explicit assertion of a oneness in the Godhead composed of three constituents. And this passage is spurious. It is acknowledged to be such by the great Trinitarian critics themselves. It would be omitted by any council of trustworthy scholars from the Protestant sects, who should be called to decide whether it should remain in the Bible. It was foisted upon an early manuscript by some partisan transcriber, who thought, most likely, that the New Testament ought to be made more emphatically Trinitarian. You will look in vain for any recognition, in what the Apostle John wrote in the epistles, of the threefold unity of the Divine nature, or the separate personality of the Holy Ghost.

And now the Book of Revelation is to be spoken of. In this tremendous poem the throne of God is described, but no Trinity is depicted as revealed from it. No Trinity is symbolized in any of its fire-sketches of the scenery and sanctities of heaven. The worship of the invisible world, the praise of angels and the redeemed, is interpreted to us in verses such as earthly pages never caught from any other pen. The Almighty and the Lamb are adored in the choruses; but they are not worshipped as one, and the Holy Spirit is not celebrated in their praise. Indeed, the book opens with these words: "The revelation of Jesus Christ which God gave unto him, to show unto his servants things which must shortly come to pass." Take notice that it is Christ in heaven, not on earth in a mortal body, of whom this dependence on God for knowledge is affirmed. And Christ is called in it "the beginning of the creation of God," "the prince of the kings of the earth." He is represented in it as saying: "To him that overcometh will I grant to sit with me in my throne, even as I also overcame, and am set down with my Father in his throne." Is this a Trinitarian book? Would a Trinitarian poet of modern times, flooded with the ecstasy of devotion, and pouring out his imaginations of heaven and its worship, presume to depict a throne over which no Trinity brooded, a sanctification independent of the third person of the Godhead, a universal hallelujah, and no breath of it lifted to the Holy Ghost?

I do not pretend, of course, that, in the books scanned thus rapidly, there are not very difficult questions to be examined as to the relations of Christ's nature and office to the Divine Love, the gift of the Divine Spirit, and the regeneration of the world. But I maintain that whatever doctrines they may teach, *they do not teach the Trinity of the church creeds of to-day*, and are fatally inconsistent with the formula of the Divine nature, which I quoted from the discourse of the Cambridge preacher, and in which he embraces the Trinity as the only Scriptural scheme. And these are documents which should not only be in harmony with it, but which should be the *sources* of it, — in which it should appear as unmistakably as in any modern creed.

We come now to the thirteen Epistles of St. Paul. Do they announce or support the ecclesiastical doctrine of the Trinity? Sitting down to an exclusive study of those letters, putting aside the interpretations and developments of later generations in the Church, have we a right to say, are we compelled to say, that nothing but the modern conception of Three Divine Persons as one God will correspond with the earliest thought and worship of the Church, so far as Paul instructed and controlled it?

Do not let us confuse points here, or be drawn to side-issues. Paul affirmed a very high doctrine of Jesus Christ. He believed and taught with fervor and joy that the spiritual life of the race was dependent on the advent of Christ from heaven, his assumption of our mortal flesh and lot, his death, resurrection and ascension. I can have no controversy with any Christian who draws this doctrine from the great Apostle. His letters affirm that Christ is to be praised and worshipped in some degree by the whole creation. But do they declare that he is God underived in his being, as Dr. Huntington says, "not subordinate in nature or essence, nor created, nor beginning, but consubstantial with the Father," so that he is to be worshipped as God? Still further, which is our special concern here, do they teach that God has revealed himself, and is to be adored as a Tri-unity, and that worship is defective which is not paid to God the Father, God the Son, and God the Holy Ghost, three persons and one Deity?

Without the slightest fear of disproof, I say, No. They make no such statement explicitly, and they do not imply such a conception. They not only do not declare or include such a doctrine, — they oppose and forbid it.

It would require a very long discourse even to state clearly, in modern language, the relations of Christ's life and his triumph over death to the doom and the redemption of humanity, as St. Paul conceived them. But we must pause a moment upon his doctrine of the

Spirit, which is inwrought with the whole web of his theology, and with his practical application of Christian truth. As a Pharisee, before his conversion to Jesus, Paul believed in God as the Monarch of nature, the distant Lord of the Hebrew nation, judging them by a law which he had published through Moses and interpreted by Prophets, promising them a national Messiah, whose rule and favor they were to deserve by ritual obedience — but not coming near to them himself, and pouring out no spiritual blessings upon the vast Gentile world. As a Christian he believed, not only that Jesus had assumed a human nature, and died to express the love of God and break the bondage of evil, but that by his ascension he had opened a perpetual fountain of grace for humanity. The Spirit of God, the very light and love which the Infinite had kept shrouded from the race before, was poured now into every soul that vitally believed in the risen Jesus. There was no abyss any more between God and man. The Divine radiance that was in Christ in his former state, and that was continued to him while in a mortal form, was now imparted to every soul that joined itself to him by gratitude and trust. So that a man, as a Christian, in Paul's view, did not pledge himself to walk by a written revelation or the recorded example of Christ, but received the inward illumination from the Divine Spirit flowing through Christ into his soul. By that Spirit we are enabled to say "Father" to God, as Christ said it on earth, and says it now in heaven. We are aided to pray: we apprehend some of the deep things of God: we discern what eye had not seen nor ear heard, nor had entered into the heart of man before: we know that we are sons of the Infinite: we are "heirs of God and joint-heirs with Christ."

Sometimes Paul calls this diffused grace the Spirit of Christ, sometimes the mind of Christ, sometimes the Spirit of God, again simply the Spirit, then the Holy Spirit, and often in our version it is rendered the Holy Ghost. It was this which gave life and unity to the Church. This was the life of God received into human nature, to cleanse, quicken, comfort, and inspire. By it the fellowship was completed between souls on earth and Christ, and the Infinite Love. "Ye are not in the flesh, but in the spirit, if so be that the Spirit of God dwell in you. And if Christ be in you, the body is dead because of sin; but the spirit is life because of righteousness. But if the spirit of him that raised up Jesus from the dead dwell in you, he that raised up Christ from the dead shall also quicken your mortal bodies by his Spirit that dwelleth in you."

Paul's doctrine of the Holy Spirit is the affirmation that the deepest divine life is communicated to human nature as a present possession by a true Christian faith, so that we are brought into organic fellowship and oneness here with Christ, and derive truth at first hand from God, not at second hand through a Bible, and at third hand through creeds or ecclesiastical corporations. It is the Quaker doctrine inflamed with a passion like Luther's. The Church has lost in great degree this meaning of it, and stumbles over the majestic sentences into the conception that they teach a separate God, mysteriously one with the Father, but distinct in consciousness, office, and will.

Dr. Neander, the most learned Christian student and

scholar of our century, himself Orthodox according to a very mild and genial type, in his history of the Planting and Training of the Christian Church, has devoted a considerable portion of the volume to a systematic exposition of St. Paul's theological scheme. He has no title over any page for the doctrine of the Trinity, thus showing that he found no such dogma as the Tripersonality of the Infinite in the domain of the Apostle's thought. But at the close of the book, in another connection, he defines Paul's essential thought to be that the Father, through the Son, dwells in mankind who are animated by his Spirit. Precisely the conception of the Holy Spirit which I have endeavored to state. This, and St. John's doctrine of the Logos, Dr. Neander, a Trinitarian, calls "the intimations" out of which the reflective intellect has sought "to elevate itself to an original triad in God."

But it may be said that the frequent use of phrases by Paul in which Father, Son, and Holy Ghost are invoked or adored, shows that he regarded them as three persons, and coequal, at least in their claim to human homage. Now without dwelling on the argument that, if Paul believed in three Divine Persons, it by no means follows that he believed them to be equal in rank, and portions of one Deity, let me ask you how frequent Paul's use of such a form of ascription or invocation is. A great many zealous Christians, regular readers of their Bibles, it can hardly be doubted, believe that such expressions occur often in the New Testament. Probably thousands of intelligent disciples would answer, "Yes," if they were asked whether the doxology, "Glory be to the Father, and to the Son, and to the Holy Ghost," is a Scriptural sentence. There is no such language between the covers of the Bible.

Indeed, it is to be feared that Dr. Huntington has not attended carefully to the testimony of the New Testament on this point. He speaks of many passages in the Gospels and Epistles that teach the separate personality of the Holy Spirit, which can be wrested from their obvious meaning only by violence. And he calls attention to "the Apostolical benedictions, which were evidently intended to be what they have so generally proved, the familiar repositories and often repeated symbols of the great central facts of Christian theology." He calls especial attention to one of these as proving the personality of the Holy Ghost. It is at the close of the second letter to the Corinthians. And how many more do you suppose there are? Not another. It is the solitary passage in the whole New Testament where Father, Son, and Holy Ghost are combined in any formal expression of worship. And this one Dr. Huntington quotes wrongly. More than that, he lays the stress of his argument on a word, which he italicizes, that does not appear in our version. He quotes it: "The grace of our Lord Jesus Christ, and the love of God, and the *fellowship* of the Holy Ghost, be with us all evermore;" and calls particular attention to the word "fellowship," as attributing to the Holy Ghost a separate consciousness and personality. But Paul said, "the communion of the Holy Ghost." It is the common partaking and consciousnesss of the Divine Spirit which he invokes for the Corinthians in connection with the grace of Christ and the love of God. This is exactly in harmony with the interpretation we have given of Paul's conception of the Spirit, as the life of God communicated to man, dwelling in each heart, and uniting the Church in a common life. Once afterwards Dr. Huntington quotes the passage in his discourse with the same error. Of course, I do not mean even to intimate that, in calling attention to the Apostolical benedictions in support of the Divine Tripersonality, when there is only one which uses the threefold element, and in wrongly quoting the vital word in that one, the writer intended to trifle with facts. Such a suspicion would be not only uncharitable, but absurd. It shows, however, the loose way in which the Scriptural evidence for the modern doctrine of the Trinity is too often studied and arranged. It is not the only instance of inaccurate citation from Scripture in the discourse. But the mistake will not be a misfortune, if it shall lead Dr. Huntington to see that he has thrown out several sneers at the manner in which those who deny the Trinity treat the evidence, and that he has not made one generous allusion to the use of Scripture by Unitarians, amongst whom he was a favorite and honored preacher for many years.

The benedictions of St. Paul, at the commencement and ending of his Epistles, and the short bursts of praise into which he rises at times in the midst of his reasoning, are *opposed* to the idea that he was a Trinitarian. "Grace to you and peace from God our Father, and the Lord Jesus Christ," — this, with the variation of a word or two, is the salutation at the commencement of all the thirteen Epistles from his pen. At their close he invokes blessings from God, or the peace of God, for his brethren, and often unites the name of Jesus in a subordinate way. But there is no address to the Holy Spirit, no supplication from the Spirit, no conjunction of Father, Son, and Spirit, in any direct homage or petition. In the one instance, out of some thirty ascriptions and benedictions, where the Spirit is introduced, the associated word implies that the Spirit is not a distinct Divine Being, but the communicated life of God to the Church. Could these facts be stated of those Epistles if they were Trinitarian documents, the fountains of the Trinitarian scheme for the whole future of Christendom? As to the spiritual life of believers, Paul uses the conception of Father, Christ, and the Spirit; for the Father communicates his Spirit — the same which Christ is filled with — to the souls of men as their light and strength. But when Paul rises into language of direct worship, he drops the Spirit from his ascriptions and prayers, because it is the Father communicated, and of course is not to be addressed as a separate Person.

But, still further, the Trinitarian dogma, so far as St. Paul is concerned, is opposed by the unequivocal terms in which he speaks of the rank of Christ. It is a very high position in the universe which the Apostle attributes to Jesus, but nothing like the rank required by the Trinitarian hypothesis. Dr. Huntington tells us that in Scripture "the Eternal Son is seen remaining rooted forever in the Godhead, having the basis of his being unchanged, deific, uncreated." No such language, and no language that has such meaning, can be drawn from the Chief Apostle. Dr. Neander confesses that Paul "ascribes a truly divine yet derived being to Christ." It is plain that Paul believed in his pre-existence, but there is no passage in which it is stated that he existed from eternity.

According to Paul he is the Son of God, not God the Son. Whether the Apostle believed the human soul was made of any different substance originally than was given to Christ, we cannot determine from his Epistles; but he certainly teaches that all really Christian persons receive into their natures the same effluence from God with which Christ is filled, and become Sons of God substantially as he is. He teaches that Christ in his pre-existent life was the highest object of the Divine affection, a love that implies dependence and a return of filial emotion and obedience. He was the image of God, the one highest and perfect form for receiving and transmitting the rays of the Infinite glory. Through him, Paul declares, God created all things; but it has been seriously doubted whether he means by this that Christ was an instrument for shaping the material world. It has been supposed that he referred rather to souls, and the plan and gradations of the moral world, celestial and earthly. This point must always remain in dispute, as there are not passages enough to settle it. But the verses in Colossians, where the statement is made with more fulness than elsewhere, favors the latter view, since, in defining the "all things" which were created by Christ, he says, "whether they be thrones, or dominions, or principalities, or powers."

There is hardly a page of St. Paul's writing that does not declare or imply a separate, and therefore finite consciousness, reason, and will in Christ, not merely when on the earth, and in a human form, but prior to his advent, and after his ascension. For it is not the doctrine of the Incarnation as ordinarily taught in the Church which Paul promulged. God did not take our nature and undergo humiliation and taste mortal woe. He expressed his love in yielding the dearest object of his unfathomable affection to the buffets and hatreds of the world and the doom of evil in the flesh. This was God's sacrifice, — "he spared not his own Son, but delivered him up for us all." And through him, the consummate form, and thus the largest channel in the universe, of the Divine Spirit, God poured redeeming life into humanity on earth.

There are two or three passages in the Pauline Epistles, of which the Greek reading or pointing is not settled among scholars, that have been made very prominent in the controversy as to the position of Jesus in the universe. Too much importance, we think, has been accorded to them. They would still be doubtful passages, if rendered as the Trinitarians demand; and doubtful passages, in unsystematic writings like the Pauline letters, must be construed in harmony with clear and positive ones. As to the power and rank of Christ, we have from Paul positive declarations concerning his origin, his resurrection and the rank received after it, and his position after the Mediatorial mission is finished, which are conclusive against the doctrine of his underived being, infinite Lordship, and Eternal coequality.

Paul tells us explicitly, in the first chapter of Colossians, that he is "the first-born of every creature." Whether this means the first-born creature of God, or first-born being before every creature, it settles the fact that Paul did not hold to the Eternal Existence of Jesus.* There is no other passage in which the Apostle deals with this question.

Second, as to the resurrection, it is always declared to have been wrought by the power of God acting upon Christ as upon a finite nature, — Christ as one unmixed personality on one hand, and God as one quickening power on the other. On the Trinitarian hypothesis, Christ should have raised himself, and ascended by the force of his native Godhead. But this is never asserted in Paul's pages, as it would have been if he had held the underived, intrinsic Deity of Christ's nature. As the letter to the Hebrews hints, so Paul seems to declare, that Jesus, as a reward for his earthly service and suffering, was lifted by the Infinite love to a greater height of glory in the heavens than before his assumption of the flesh. For the Apostle speaks to the Ephesians of the working of God's mighty power, "which he wrought in Christ when he raised him from the dead, and set him at his own right hand in the heavenly places, far above all principality, and power, and might, and dominion, and every name that is named, not only in this world, but also in that which is to come." And once more, to the Philippians, after

---

* As Tertullian wrote, perhaps with this passage in view, in the third century, before such Orthodoxy as that of the New England standards had been dreamed: "God is both a Father, and also a Judge, yet not therefore always a Father and a Judge because always God. Since neither could he be a Father before a Son, nor a Judge before Sin; but there was a time when both Sin and Son were not, which make the Lord a Judge and Father."

referring to his death on the cross, he says, "*Wherefore*, God also hath highly exalted him, and given him a name which is above every name; that at the name of Jesus every knee should bow, of things in heaven, and things in earth, and things under the earth; and that every tongue should confess that Jesus Christ is Lord, to the glory of God the Father."

Dr. Huntington quotes from the first of these passages, and asks, "Can this be a creature?" What else, we answer, if he was raised from the dead by God's power, and lifted to the position far above "all principality and power," &c.? He quotes part of the second passage, and exclaims, "Is not this a being to whom prayer is to be offered?" Praise certainly, Paul would answer him, if it be offered "to the glory of God the Father," and not to an underived, coequal Infinite. If he were that, it would not be said that God had highly exalted him. For it is not the human nature, but the veritable soul of Christ, that is thus exalted. It is after the resurrection, when the flesh and its limitations are put off.

And thirdly, Paul expressly tells us what the *final* relation of Jesus to God is to be, after every knee has bowed to him. In the 15th chapter of the first letter to the Corinthians, he speaks of the resurrection and the close of Christ's administrative office. "Then cometh the end, when he shall have delivered up the kingdom to God, even the Father. . . . . . And when all things shall be subdued unto him, then shall the Son also himself be subject unto him that put all things under him, that God may be all in all." If Scripture alone were the source of our creeds, can one think it possible that modern Trinitarianism could survive this passage? Christ becomes visibly subject forever, and God the Father is all in all! Dr. Huntington quotes this passage, and thus explains it: "The Son, in his character of Sonship, is retaken, so to speak, into the everlasting, almighty, ineffable, undivided One, where the distinctions of office which had aided us so greatly in apprehending the glorious Trinity are lost to our sight." This is the most astounding specimen of exegesis which has ever fallen under my observation. Those that tamper with Scripture by rationalistic dissections are generally referred, by strict Orthodox believers, to the woes denounced at the close of the Book of Revelation against those who add to or take from the words of the book. Where is anything said or suggested in 15th Corinthians about the melting away of the Trinity, and the reabsorption of the Son into the absolute Godhead? It is fiction. With such license as that, a man might go through Scripture and strike out every instance where "not" occurs, thus reversing the morals of the New Testament. In fact, Dr. Huntington does precisely reverse the sense of Paul by his interpretation, or rather metamorphosis, of the passage. Paul says that Christ stands higher in administrative rank before the close of his mediatorship than he will afterwards. Dr. Huntington makes him say that he stands lower now, and is to go higher then. Or rather, he makes Paul say, that the Christ, known once on earth, is to be annihilated; for when the Son is retaken into the undivided Godhead, where is the once visible Christ to be found? Of course, Trinitarianism requires some such wrenching of this clear and fatal statement of Paul. And yet only on the third page after this handling of the Unitarian Apostle's affirmation, we find Dr. Huntington, in reference to a Unitarian theory of the Holy Spirit which he does not fairly state, exclaiming, "How desperate the shifts of a determined theory!"

We have thus grouped and surveyed the evidence afforded by the books of the New Testament for the doctrine of the Trinity. Of course, within such restricted limits, it has been impossible to treat any portion of the subject in an exhaustive way. But I have carefully abstained from any excessive statement in presenting the testimony as it had revealed itself to my reading. And perhaps a better conception can be gained of the quality and force of the warrant or opposition in regard to the doctrine by a general outlook over its field, than by microscopic scrutiny of passages drawn at random from its various books. We can tell in such a way, at once, whether any passages jut up from the broad landscape of its teachings, compelling us to accept the Trinity of God as its dominant idea and revelation.

We have found no such passages there. There is no such word as Trinity in its chapters. There is no statement that the unity of God is composed of three elements or personalities, or diverges into three forms. None of the words or phrases in which Dr. Huntington clothes his faith, or in which any Orthodox Trinitarianism has been or can be defined, is to be found in its whole compass (with the exception of one verse, confessed by Trinitarians to be spurious). The words "Triune name" are not there, nor "Three in one," nor

"Eternal Son," nor "consubstantial," nor "equal in power and glory" applied to God and Christ and the Holy Spirit, nor "rooted forever in the Godhead," nor "God the Son," nor "Very God of Very God," nor "Light of Light," nor "eternally begotten of the Father," nor "coequal persons," nor "threefold distinction." There is no offering of praise to Father, Son, and Holy Ghost, and no direct address to them in any formula of invocation or appeal. The last document of the New Testament, the Gospel of John, was written about as late as the year 100, so that the Christian Church had then been nearly seventy years — two generations — under the guidance of Apostolic teaching; and yet no combination of words appears in the compass of the New Testament books, such as is required to be signed in every Orthodox theological school of Christendom, and is expected in the ascriptions and doxologies of worship in the vast majority of the churches of all lands. A man has to go outside the Bible for all the expressions in which Dr. Huntington announces the foundation of his newly-acquired faith. And if a man says, "I believe in the Bible; I accept the whole of the New Testament; but do not believe in the Tripersonality of God;" the theologian who pronounces his faith unsound, or incomplete, must set up not merely his *interpretations* of the Bible, but his bold, explicit *additions* to it, as the tests of truth and fellowship.

Dr. Huntington in one passage of his discourse, the most emphatic passage in it, for he prints it all in italics, after speaking of some of the declarations in the New Testament concerning Jesus, requests a Unitarian to put this question to himself: — "*Whatever I may make these words mean now, would they ever have been chosen and used in the first place on any other belief than that Christ is properly and truly Divine, Eternal, Almighty, as the Church of his Heaven-guided people has believed and taught?"* We take up this challenge, deliberately and without hesitation. We *seek* its test, and we reverse its statement precisely. We say the Scriptural affirmations and omissions, as we have quoted or stated them, are such that they could not possibly have been made by teachers who believe, with the modern Protestant Church, that Christ is one of three persons in the Godhead, and that he is Eternal and Almighty, or of higher rank than the appointed medium and minister of Infinite Grace to souls who are to partake of his very substance, and be sons of God in fellowship with him.

The doctrine of the Triunity is *not* a doctrine of the New Testament. Some of the wisest Trinitarian scholars and theologians have confessed that it cannot be derived, in any of its accepted and required forms to-day, from the express language of the Evangelists and Apostles. They confess that it must be reasoned out, inferred, developed from intimations in the New Testament. *Intimations!* That is, when the doctrine first broke upon the awe-struck souls of men who had been Unitarians before, they did not state it clearly; they did not state at all that there are three equal Divine beings; they did not utter in any logical, lyrical, impassioned, or reverential sentence, that those three are one! The most learned Church historian of modern times, Dr. Neander, of Germany, has not hesitated to speak of the Trinity which is now maintained, as an idea to which the reflective mind has sought to elevate itself, rather than a clear publication of the Bible. Dr. Huntington quotes this admirable man as declaring that the doctrine of the Trinity is the fundamental article of the Christian faith, — the essential contents of Christianity summed up in brief. This is another instance of a strange carelessness in the use of authorities, in which Dr. Huntington, writing a discourse so important, should not have indulged himself. Dr. Neander does say that *he recognizes* in the doctrine of the Trinity "the essential contents of Christianity, summed up in brief," that is, summed up in human phrase and shaping; but he expressly states on the same page, (History of the Christian Religion and Church, Vol. I. p. 572,) three sentences before this declaration, exactly the opposite of Prof. Huntington's quotation. He says: "This doctrine does not belong to the fundamental articles of the Christian faith; as appears sufficiently evident from the fact, that it is expressly held forth in no one particular passage of the New Testament; for the only one in which this is done, the passage relating to the three that bear record (1 John v. 7), is undoubtedly spurious, and in its ungenuine shape testifies to the fact, how foreign such a collocation is from the style of the New Testament Scriptures. We find in the New Testament no other fundamental article besides that of which the Apostle Paul says, that other foundation can no man lay than that is laid, the annunciation of Jesus as the Messiah; and Christ himself designates as the foundation of his religion the faith in the only true God, and in Jesus Christ whom he hath sent."* Dr. Nean-

---

* While these pages are passing through the press, we notice that attention has been called by a well-known and accurate scholar, through the columns of the "Christian Register" of January

der was a Trinitarian, — of a very different type, however, from the common American Trinitarians. He believed that his doctrine of the Trinity is properly developed out of the Bible. But in his judgment it is there so dim and latent, that it cannot be accounted a fundamental article of the Christian religion. We leave that point to be settled between the first volume of his Church History and Dr. Huntington, who has unfortunately, but of course not intentionally, misquoted it; while we repeat our affirmation that the doctrine as now held, and as interpreted by Prof. Huntington, is not only not clearly stated in the New Testament; — the elements of it are not there; — and that it is impossible it could be there at all, crowded as those pages are with references to God, and Christ, and the Spirit of God, unless it should lie there clear as the sunlight, as clear at least as the creeds of Christendom.

I have no time and no desire to follow Dr. Huntington in the argument he has made to show how necessary the doctrine of the Trinity is to the other salient features of the Orthodox theology. Perhaps it is necessary. If it falls, very likely the modern interpretation of the Atonement and Divine government must fall. If so, it is only necessary to consider the Scriptural sources for that doctrine, and the work of criticism upon modern Orthodoxy is accomplished.

21st, to this mistake of Dr. Huntington in quoting from Neander. The accomplished critic shows also, that, in the American translation of Neander, the word "strictly" is introduced into the text, thus weakening a little the force of Neander's declaration. The American version makes the passage read, "This doctrine does not *strictly* belong to the fundamental articles of the Christian faith," while Neander wrote unqualifiedly, "This doctrine does not belong," &c.

But I must say a word, before closing, upon two or three intimations in Dr. Huntington's discourse concerning the method of testing the Scripture evidence for the Trinity. It is often affirmed by Orthodox theologians, that opposition of the heart, hostility to divine grace, blinds the intellect to the evidence in the Bible for the Deity of Christ and the Trinity of the Godhead. This position is one of amazing arrogance; yes, I am ready to say, of intolerable insolence. Used by one student of the Bible to another, in a course of serious investigation as to the teaching of Scripture, it is an insult as manifest as the smiting of the face, or any other gross personal indignity. For one I will never allow it for a moment, from any man who addresses to me an argument, or with whom I am conducting an honest discussion.

It surprised and pained me, in reading Dr. Huntington's discourse, to find him verging to this position, and using language, now and then, that can hardly be construed into any other significance. He speaks of seeing the truth of Christ's Deity in Scripture, "which was lying all the time plain and persuasive to the eye," "through a happier admission of God's grace," and declares that, to all the ordinary objections of science and logic, the believer has only to answer, "I know in whom I have believed," and then may quote such words as "the natural man receiveth not the things of the Spirit of God, because they are spiritually discerned." In a previous volume, "Sermons for the People," page 265, a similar indignity is offered to Unitarian students of Scripture by the contemptuous and insufferable statement that our interpretations of passages that refer to Christ "will satisfy, till some special exigency of spiritual experience dissolves them in its potent alembic."

Does Dr. Huntington mean that the constitution of the Godhead, whether the Infinite is one or three, is a question to be spiritually discerned? Is he willing, or not, to stand by the fair, full, exhaustive testimony of Scripture, logically distributed and combined? And when none of the words, affirmations, praises, or prayers, demanded by the Trinity, are found in the New Testament, the fountain of all our external authority for testing what Christianity is, will he retreat from the terrific force of the facts, and advise a partisan of the doctrine to retreat into the position, that he knows, *internally*, that Christ never began to be, — that he is sure, by an *inward* witness, that the Godhead is composed of

"God the Father, God the Son,
And God the Spirit, three in one"?

This is what his expressions mean, if they mean anything. Let us refuse to believe that he deliberately puts such an unmanly, arrogant sense into them, but that they are used loosely, with no intention of affirming so gross and repulsive an assumption.

The doctrine of Trinity, or strict unity, is an external doctrine, to be tested by the logical meaning of Scripture. An abandoned man, if his intellect is clear, and his reason unprejudiced, is competent to decide that question. Spiritual things are spiritually discerned. But spiritual things, brethren, belong alike to Trinitarian and Unitarian schemes of faith. They are the internal things of our poor dogmas. And by the inward eye, and the sensitive spiritual affections, we come into the communion of the Spirit, the fellowship of Christ, the love of the Father, though we never can harmonize their relations logically, in a conception of the Infinite Being.

DR. HUNTINGTON ON THE TRINITY.

[From the Monthly Religious Magazine, February, 1860.]

WE have endeavored to give our readers, in another department of the Magazine,* a view of Dr. Huntington's argument in favor of the tripersonality of the object of Christian worship. Many of them will read the volume itself, and see the argument in its whole breadth and fulness. The main points are the following.

The doctrine of the Trinity, or rather Tripersonality, for that is the form which it assumes in his statement, and the two terms are by no means synonymous, has with trifling exceptions been held by Christian believers ever and everywhere. Though truth is not determined by majorities, yet it is hardly credible that the great Head of the Church, who promised to be with it always, would suffer it to embrace a delusion so wide-spread, and running through all the ages. To suppose this is painful, not to say irreverent towards the Providence that has ever led and watched the true Christian Israel.

This doctrine, or the system of which it forms a part, is essential to render Christianity practically an efficient and vital power in the world and in the human soul. Leave this out, and man fails to see the extent of sin

---

* See Magazine for February, 1860, page 130.

and its terrible evil; piety wastes, the Church declines, enthusiasm is chilled, prayer loses its efficacy, and the world reaps an easy harvest. Restore it, and the Church becomes aggressive; the sinner is convinced and finds peace in believing, and devotion revives again.

This doctrine, and the system to which it belongs, give unity to the Bible, and make all its disclosures and utterances fall into one majestic and consistent plan. From Genesis to the Apocalypse, the great themes of Incarnation and Redemption are all-harmonizing and make all difficulties of exegesis to vanish, while to the Anti-Trinitarian they are insurmountable, or require unnatural or labored explanations.

These three heads seem to us to sum up the argument, which in the Sermon is drawn out in various detail, and with great rhetorical skill. This doctrine of threeness in the Divine Nature has been the almost universally accepted one through all the ages of faith: it is necessary in order to make Christianity an efficient, working, and renewing power; and it makes the Bible a consistent and symmetrical whole.

These tests, if they would bear examination, would certainly be conclusive. To present them fairly and plainly, rather than to controvert them, is our purpose now. But as this is not our view of the Christian history, economy, and revelation, and as the whole subject goes to the very life and essence of Christianity, and the deeps of the Christian experience, we ask the company of our readers while we take them, not into another controversy about the Trinity, but to some points of observation, from which in a light somewhat different this great field of truth may lie before us.

I. It is a pretty sure indication of corruption in theology when its service requires of us to wrest language from its legitimate use, and employ it in the Church as Talleyrand did in the State, to conceal or to obscure thought rather than reveal it. Dr. Huntington does not consciously do this, but any system of tripersonality must. Everybody has an idea, till it is dissipated by metaphysics, of what a person is. A person is an individual being, having his own separate self-consciousness; and to be personally known to us, he must be revealed to us in living form. To say that God exists in three persons is to say that there are three self-conscious beings, and the conception is produced instantly in the mind of three Gods. You may protest that you are not using language in its common acceptation; but what does the protest avail, if you go right on and assign to the three persons such offices and functions as inevitably beget the notion of three self-conscious actors in the believer's mind? Is it the words on your lips, or is it the inmost thought of your heart, that God regards in worship? We may say "one God" with the mouth all day and all night, and yet if the attitude of the soul within is towards three Persons each with an "independent self-consciousness," and each having Divine attributes, then the motions of the mouth are as empty sounds, while the act of the soul is an unblest idolatry.

The doctrine of threeness in the Divine Nature is held now, and has been held from remote ages, by those who do not divide the Divine Personality. We never can know anything of God, except so far as he becomes humanized to our human conceptions. This seems plain. Man is his image and partakes of his nature. All that we say of God, his mercy, his justice, his holiness, his goodness, mean nothing to us, except so far forth as there is something in our own being that answers to those great ideas. Just so likewise of his unity, his threeness, and his personality. There is ground for these in our own nature, or we could not even receive a revelation respecting them. Man's nature is triune. He is love, intellect, and active power: heart, head, hand; — as Sir William Hamilton puts it in his clear and masterly analysis, feeling, cognition, and conation: the sole ground in man whence he can arise to the august conception of the Divine Threeness, — the eternal Love, the eternal Wisdom or Word, and their eternal processions of Power. We may strain after something about God when there is nothing in man to receive it: it will not even fall within the laws of thought; we only beat the air and hear the "clatter" of our own intellectual machinery. That God is Love, Wisdom, and Power, all existing in one self-conscious being or person, creating man for feeling, knowing, and doing, comes at once into our faith that puts us in communion with the Supreme in just the degree that we will suffer him to mould us into his own glorious image.

II. It is the concession of candid Trinitarians that the Tripersonality is not found expressly in the New Testament, but was "developed" afterwards by the Christian Church. "This doctrine does not strictly belong to the fundamental articles of the Christian faith, as appears sufficiently evident from the fact that it is expressly held forth in no one particular passage of the New Testament," is the language of Neander.

"The unfolding of the mystery is committed to the scientific activity of the Church," is the language of Olshausen. But that the doctrine of Christ's essential divinity is set forth in the New Testament, yea, that it breaks from its pages in a blaze of glory, is the almost unanimous agreement of Christian believers. In the Incarnation, the Life, and the Mediation of Christ there is the full expression of the Godhead, the essential Divinity coming down into visible personality for the salvation of man. Never are we invited to come to the Father by climbing round the personality of the Son. That there are eternal deeps of the Divine Nature that we may never fathom, is only saying that we are weak and finite. That all which we can know or understand of God we have in Christ, the incarnate and revealing Word, is his own declaration again and again. "No man hath seen God at any time; the only-begotten Son that dwelleth in the bosom of the Father, he hath declared him." "*All that the Father hath is mine.*" "He that hath seen me hath seen the Father." That the essential Divinity in Christ is not a person separated from the Father, another person, but consubstantial with the Father, and revealing the whole Godhead in one glorious person, "*all* the fulness of the Godhead bodily," is plain even in the letter; but in the only system of interpretation self-consistent throughout, — we mean the New Church law of analogies, — this central truth of the New Testament appears like the sun shining in his strength.

And mark with what plainness the Holy Spirit is described as the gift of Christ, the procession of life and power coming from him alone: "*He* shall baptize you with the Holy Spirit and with fire." "*I* will send you another Comforter, even the Spirit of truth." "He breathed on them, saying, 'Receive ye the Holy Spirit.'" The exigencies of theology must be hard-pressing indeed, that can turn this sweet and blessed doctrine aside, of a cleansing and comforting power pulsing into the soul from a Divine Saviour, brought near to the disciple by personal communion and lowly faith, for that strange riddle of the understanding, a third person in the Trinity coming and going between God and man!

III. The first historical development of Christianity was in strict accordance with this conception of one God in one person, and that person brought near to man in the Divine Saviour. The Pentecostal scene fulfilled the promise of the Comforter. It was not produced by preaching Tripersonality and a vicarious atonement. It was produced by preaching Christ and the resurrection with repentance and remission of sins; and as for the Holy Spirit which came as a baptism of fire, it was said of the glorified Saviour, "*He* hath shed forth this which ye now see and hear." So the first conversions were made and the first churches were built up. When Paul looked up through the opened heavens, and sought the source of that power which smote him to the earth and overwhelmed him with self-convictions, the answer was, "I am Jesus of Nazareth whom thou persecutest." They called on the name of the Lord Jesus, and the Holy Spirit came. It was the Divine Sphere of Light and Love and Power brought down to the earth in the Lord Jesus Christ, and turned full upon man. The "scientific activity" of the Church had not yet begun. They simply looked up to the Saviour, the God become man, and "the Holy Ghost fell on them," (a person indeed?) and its power rolled in upon them in surges of energy, peace, and love. And when John was "in the Spirit," and saw the glorious Theophany, did he see three persons each claiming divine honors, or did he see "one like unto the Son of Man," saying, "I am the First and the Last, which is, and which was, and which is to come, the Almighty"?

No student of history, we think, will affirm that there is the least hint of tripersonality in the Godhead in the writings extant of the Apostolic Fathers. Later down, from A. D. 175 to 200, we have explicit statements from Justin Martyr, Irenæus, and Tertullian of the essentials of the Christian faith, and what had "always been believed" in the Church. In these the essential Divinity of Christ is fully and affectionately acknowledged, the New Testament form, both of language and doctrine, is preserved; but there is no lisp of tripersonality or a substitutive atonement. These old creeds are refreshing, for they have the breath of the morning hour. Irenæus gives the following as the creed of those "who diligently keep the ancient tradition": "Believing in one God, maker of Heaven and earth, and of all things in them by Christ Jesus the Son of God, who through his most eminent love towards his creature underwent that generation which was of a virgin, He by himself uniting man to God, and having suffered under Pontius Pilate and being rose again and taken up in splendor will come again in glory, a Saviour of them that are saved and a judge of them that are judged, sending into eternal fire the perverters of truth, and the despisers of his Father, and of his own coming again." Tertullian gives the following as "the rule that had been observed and adhered to from the very beginning of the Gospel,"—that it was "prior to all heretics that had been in the Christian Church." He believed "in one God, and that his Word was the Son of the one God; who proceeded from him; by whom all things were made, and without whom nothing was made; that he was sent by or from the Father into the virgin, and from her was born Man and God, the Son of Man and the Son of God, and named Jesus Christ; that he suffered, that he died, that he was buried according to the Scriptures, and raised up by the Father, and, taken up into heaven, sits at the right hand of the Father, and will come to judge the quick and the dead; who from thence sent, according to his promise from the Father, the Holy Ghost, the Paraclete, the Sanctifier of their faith who believe in the Father and Son and Holy Ghost."

That in this conception of Father and Son they did not separate the Divine Nature into persons, appears from the following explanation of Tertullian: "Before all things, God was alone; but not absolutely alone, for he had with him his own reason, since God is a rational being. This reason the Greeks call Logos, which word we now render Sermo. AND THAT YOU MAY MORE EASILY UNDERSTAND THIS FROM YOURSELF, CONSIDER THAT YOU WHO ARE MADE IN THE IMAGE OF GOD HAVE REASON WITHIN YOURSELF."*

---

* But Tertullian "developed" the doctrine of the Logos in

IV. But "the scientific activity of the Church" was at hand. Precisely in the degree that it declined in godliness, and the primal graces disappeared, was the Divine Personality cloven and separated in its authorized formulas. The Arian controversy raged for more than half a century, in which the worst passions were unloosed on both sides. What a surface do these times present, from which to reflect the divine doctrines, — this surging sea of human hatred and strife! The Athanasians ejected from the primitive creed the doctrine of Divine Unity, and two persons began to appear.

---

opposition to the Monarchians, and grazed the borders of Tritheism, taking ground from which his successors developed it still farther. He is the transition point between Christian Monotheism and Tripersonalism, and might be claimed either way. Among other analogies, he compares the Logos proceeding out of the Divine Essence, and becoming incarnate in Christ, to a stalk from its root, both one in substance but numerically distinct, and the Holy Spirit to the fruit upon the stalk, continuously produced through the Son. Yet again he says, that each of the three may be called God, though he does not seem to conceive of each as having "an independent self-consciousness." Neander represents, with admirable truthfulness, that the unlearned among the laity, — or, as Tertullian says, "all simple persons, not to say ignorant and illiterate, who form always the majority of believers," — in whose Christian consciousness the doctrine of Christ's divinity was the most intensely wrought, revolted against the logomachists, and would only see the whole Godhead in Christ. They would not receive at first the "developed" theology of the metaphysicians, "pervaded by reflection and dialectic distinctions." Whether these "simple persons," with an intense Christian consciousness of a present Saviour, or the learned logomachists and wranglers, were the more likely to be right, is a question which admits of a difference of opinion. See Neander's *Antignostikus*, Part III. Sec. 2.

The Arians ejected the doctrine of the Saviour's essential Divinity, and God receded into the dim and inaccessible heavens. Which party was to prevail was long doubtful. The Church split into nearly two equal factions, and it seemed a drawn battle, except as one or the other allied itself with the civil power. At length the Tripersonalists prevailed. *How* they prevailed, and by what process the ancient Anti-Trinitarianism "died out," involve a very interesting passage of history, and one which is calculated to make a man exceedingly modest in urging an argument from the "quod semper, quod ubique, quod ab omnibus."

In the year 379, Theodosius ascended the throne of the eastern division of the Roman empire. He was surnamed "the Great," and he well deserves the further addition of the Bloody and Cruel. Not that he was any worse than Roman emperors in general. He was not so bad, for he never murdered his own wife, brothers, or children, as other good Christian emperors were in the habit of doing. He had great energy of character, was thoroughly orthodox, and was amply accomplished in all the bull-dog virtues. An insurrection from a trivial cause broke out, and was soon quelled, at Thessalonica. The Emperor ordered from his officers seven thousand human heads to expiate the crime. The populace were invited into the circus; men, women, and children assembled expecting to witness the games. They were then shut in, and the butchery went on for three hours, till the seven thousand heads had been obtained. This was the man who undertook to settle disputes in theology.

The Arians were in possession of the Eastern

churches. The Patriarch at Constantinople, the monks, the clergy, and the people, were generally of that faith. The odosius did not trouble himself to examine it. He selected two prelates, Damasus, Bishop of Rome, and Peter, Bishop of Alexandria, and declared them the "treasures of true doctrine." Those whose faith conformed to theirs were orthodox, all others were to be rejected as outcasts. Fifteen edicts were issued successively, continually increasing in severity, till the heretics were hunted unto death. The Arians were driven, not only from the Church, but from their homes, and languished and died in exile; "inquisitors of the faith" were appointed to act as spies and judges of the secret opinions of men. The orthodox bishops fanned the flame of persecution. St. Gregory was installed as the new Patriarch of Constantinople, in defiance of the whole flock instrusted to his care. The brutal soldiery attended in the cathedral to force the new bishop upon the people. Pagans and Arians alike were hunted down. The pagan peasants sometimes resisted only to be butchered on the spot. On one occasion the saints declared, and the judges admitted, that, in the slaughter within the pagan temples, devils and angels entered into the combat, and the idolaters merely shared the fate of the infernal spirits with whom they were leagued. Uniformity of faith followed. Tripersonality became, if not the "quod semper," yet undoubtedly the "quod ubique, quod ab omnibus."[*]

Then followed the long, dreary, arctic night of the Church. The litanies went up to three persons, and

---

[*] Sismondi's Fall of the Roman Empire, pp. 110-112.

along with them the half-stifled groans and half-muffled cries of oppressed and weary human nature. From the cold regions or burning sands of exile, from souls slain under the altar, from the midst of blazing fagots, from dungeons under ground, from "the Alpine mountains cold," went up the prayer, "O Lord, how long!" while from all the cathedrals, churches, and monasteries went up the worship of Tritheism.

"But we must remember that the age was dark." The age undoubtedly was dark, and a very pertinent question arises, — WHAT MADE THE AGES DARK? Any age becomes dark just in the degree that the knowledge of God is lost. Any age is dark in proportion as its worship becomes untrue. The idea of God is vital, central; all our other ideas are fitted to it and borrow their light from it, as the planets replenish their light and trick their beams from the sun. All our notions of man, of duty, of neighborly love, of nature and revelation, of this life and the next, of regeneration, redemption, and preparation for heaven, are determined and vitalized by our conception of God, for that is the inmost of all our thoughts and actions. Let God be one, clear-shining, ever near, and melting into the soul, and conjunction with him is unbroken, and worship is all-renewing; all other doctrine falls into its true place and order, and there is unity everywhere else. Let our idea of the One Infinite Person be lost or blurred and dissipated, and there is darkness or lurid twilight on all the landscapes of the mind, and there is no such worship or unison with the Lord as cleanses away the foul depravity of human nature. Thus the Christian idea of God, sinking down into the ages, gathered their darkness about it deeper and deeper, and was dissipated and divided and ended in confirmed Tritheism; and then there was pagan night over all the Church, and man was a wolf to man.

We have not time to trace the influence of Tritheism on the religion of modern Protestantism, but we think it has been disastrous enough. Under Protestantism it allied itself organically with the doctrine of justification by faith alone, or putative instead of genuine righteousness, and thereby preserved all its power to hurt and to kill. To this we owe all the lurking and deadly Antinomianism of Protestantism, which these three hundred years has separated faith from charity, religion from life, ritual from goodness, and devotion from honesty. Perhaps, if we summoned all the facts to bear witness, we might hurt the oil and the wine of neighborly kindness. They are patent enough in the history of the sects; — the stakes where the martyrs have died, the dungeons on whose impassive walls their prayers have been written; the Scotland heaths lifting up their hymns amid the wildness of nature with alarms lest the hunters might hear; the Bunhill fields where the victims only found peace; the death-penalties on the statute-book wiped off within the memory of living men;* Arminianism mingling its blood with its sacrifice in all the by-ways of Holland; the half-suppressed history of the Familists, the Baptists, and the Quakers of New England; the maxims of trade and commerce and bargaining perverted, Mammon ruling in splendid

---

* Unitarianism up to a period comparatively recent was punishable with death in England. It was also punishable with death under Puritan law.

churches, and starving women in sound of their bells, stitching at ninepence a day, and stitching their own shrouds; American slavery creeping into the churches, and up to the altar and the pulpit, and overshadowing both with a deadly Atheism; the hard Jewish bearing of the sects towards each other; — these, and ten thousand more, are swift and sharp-tongued witnesses to the results of the fundamental dogma of Protestantism, which separates religion from life, and under which the sweet and heavenly charities are blasted and withered.

"The times were dark, and human rights were not understood." What made them dark, and what is it that separates man from God, and by consequence man from his brother?

V. In days of darkest corruption, and amid the most awful wickedness of an apostate Church, there have been multitudes who have lived and died in the sanctity of a genuine faith. And what has been the doctrine which has laid hold upon them and saved them? We believe it will be found to have been the essential Divinity of the Lord Jesus Christ, breaking clear of the tangles of Tritheism, and offering the Divine Person to the humble believer. This has been the saving element which no corruptions could completely overlay. It is a personal, vital union of the disciple with his Saviour that causes the Divine Life to pass into him and transform him into the Divine image, and produce from within outwardly, not a putative, but a genuine righteousness: it is this which saves him when it becomes dominant over the divided worship of Tritheism. Here in fact is the distinctive and renewing power of the Gospel. Thus Dr. Huntington writes in his Sermon on "the Secret of the New Name," and with an affecting truthfulness which in our judgment nullifies every syllable of his argument for the Tripersonality: —

"The special character and privilege of the Christian rest in a personal and conscious union between him and his living Redeemer. We vex our ingenuity straining after definitions of the distinctive thing in Christianity. They are all superficial and irrelévant compared with this. How uniform and majestic the testimony that rises from all the lands and ages of faith to this simple truth, — that it is not rules of conduct, not systems of ethics, not patterns of propriety, not eloquent expositions, that inspire the believing and faithful heart with its immortal energy and peace, but the simple secret assurance of being at one with the Lord Jesus, and resting in his almighty friendship! Where is the fiery furnace deep enough to burn despair into our souls, if we can see walking with us through the fire the form of the Son of God? What then is the tribulation, or famine, or sword, or nakedness which shall separate us from the love of God in Christ Jesus our Lord. The mystery of that unity where He who is at one with God yet cried, 'Not as I will, but as thou wilt,' is not for us to understand. Yet the prayer of promise, 'They shall be with me where I am,' is for us to lay hold of, and breathe again and again when we are aching and alone and troubled."

Not only when we are aching and alone and troubled. When we are weak or cowardly in the face of duty, or braced up only by the pride of self or the fear of man, it is rest in that almighty friendship that gives both the docility of the child and the strength of a multitude of martyrs. There is other virtue which is hardy and brave, austere, and sometimes cruel, for the cause and the glory of God. This from the living and indwelling Christ has both the tenderness and omnipotence of Him who breathes it into us, for its strain of acknowledgment is, "Thy gentleness hath made me great." This, and not the Tripersonality, has been the renewing power of Christianity, and wrought all the graces and the righteousness and the zeal and the piety distinctively Christian, for this is where God meets the soul and has his tabernacle with man. This is the door through which he comes and floods the heart with his strength and love. This made Methodism a saving and regenerating power, while the other churches lay high and dry on the sands of faith alone. It works the deepest and the richest Christian experience. It breathes and quivers through Moravian hymns. It shows man all the depths and windings of his depravity, and in the same measure supplies God's inexhaustible grace. It gives him the peace that rolls in like a river, and fertilizes all his nature as earthly fountains are becoming dry. It gives the Christian Church all the efficiency which it has for positive good in society. And when the hosts above sing "Worthy is the Lamb that was slain," — the Divine Humanity denied on earth but acknowledged in heaven, — it is this vital conscious connection between Christ and his redeemed that inspires the "hallelujahs and harping symphonies."

The argument for any doctrine based merely upon its prevalence is always suspicious, when we consider the tendencies of a corrupt human nature to bring down Divine truth to its own level. But when we lay our finger upon a doctrine which has been the animus of the Church through all its most fearful apostasies, the argument from its prevalence is blown into atoms. History as well as reason turns full against it. The temptation is strong and subtle to yield to the corrupt currents of opinion, and be swept along with them; but that we are going back to the ages when Tritheism shut over the Church like an iron cover, and shut in the darkness, there is no reason to apprehend. For one hundred years Tritheism has been less and less the organific centre of Christian theology, while the Lord Jesus Christ, as the Divine Incarnation, the descended Word, the God with men, has become such more and more. This becomes the theme of all that Christian revivalism that leaves in the renovated heart the fragrancy of heaven; and there are omens enough, if we will but see them, that not a divided worship, but a Divine Christology, shall fulfil the prediction, "Behold, the tabernacle of God is with men, and he will dwell with them, and they shall be his people, and God himself shall be with them and be their God. And God shall wipe away all tears from their eyes; and there shall be no more death, neither sorrow nor crying, neither shall there be any more pain; for the former things are passed away.

COMMUNICATIONS TO THE CHRISTIAN REGISTER,

FROM JAN. 21 TO MARCH 3, 1860; INCLUDING LETTERS BY E. A., R. P. S., AND DR. HUNTINGTON.

I.

DR. HUNTINGTON'S MISQUOTATION OF NEANDER ON THE TRINITY.

Mr. Editor: — In Dr. Huntington's Sermon on the Trinity, in his recently published volume entitled "Christian Believing and Living," he represents the doctrine of three coequal persons in the Godhead, to each of whom Divine worship is to be offered, as "the fundamental article of Christian belief," "the one essential, characteristic truth of the Christian religion." This doctrine he regards our Saviour as announcing, with the greatest solemnity, in the so-called formula of baptism, Matt. xxviii. 19, and thus giving it to his Church as its creed. (See pp. 355 – 364.) It is not my purpose here to remark on the extraordinary process which extracts the ecclesiastical dogma of the Trinity from the simple mention of the Father, the Son, and the Holy Spirit, as the primary objects of Christian faith, a public profession of which was made by baptism; nor on the peculiar state of mind which finds a proof of the *deity* of Christ in the words which precede, " All power is *given* unto me in heaven and in earth." (See pp. 366, 407, 527.) I only wish at this time to call attention to a strange, though, I doubt not, wholly unintentional misquotation and misrepresentation of Neander, by which he is made to express an opinion respecting the importance of the doctrine of the Trinity in accordance with that of Dr. Huntington, but in direct contradiction to his own. Dr. Huntington (p. 378) represents him as saying of the doctrine of the Trinity, "It is the fundamental article of the Christian faith, — the essential contents of Christianity summed up in brief."

Now the fact is, not only that Neander, though a Trinitarian, makes no such statement as Dr. Huntington here ascribes to him, but that on the very page from which this professed quotation is taken, he expressly says, and insists at length on the fact, that "the doctrine of the Trinity does *not* belong to the fundamental articles of the Christian faith." (Hist. of the Christian Religion and Church, Vol. I. p. 572, Torrey's translation.) And he does not say, that "the doctrine of the Trinity *is* the essential contents of Christianity;" he only "recognizes the essential contents of Christianity. *in* the doctrine," as constituting its practical part. These two statements are very far from equivalent. The doctrine of the Trinity *includes* the essential elements of Christianity, as husks include the ear, or as wheat may be included in a collection of chaff. Dr. Huntington's great mistake, throughout his sermon, consists in supposing that it is these husks, this chaff, that have constituted the nutriment of the Christian Church and sustained its life in all the ages past, and that we must swallow these or perish. Neander, on the other hand, never loses sight of the distinction between the grand, vital, inspiring truths concerning the Father, the Son, and the Holy Spirit, which belong to the substance of Christianity, in which *Trinitarians and Unitarians alike agree*, — and those metaphysical *speculations* upon them which have been embodied in the ecclesiastical doctrine of the Trinity, in the widely different forms in which it has at different times been held. The former he calls "the *practical* doctrine of the Trinity," or "the Trinity of revelation;" the latter he speaks of as "the speculative or ontological." He does not identify the *foundation* of the Christian religion, laid by God himself, with the "gold, silver, and precious stones," or "wood, hay, and stubble," as the case may be, which man has built upon it.

In confirmation and illustration of what has been said, I now propose, Mr. Editor, to lay before your readers the principal part of the paragraph from which Dr. Huntington has taken this strangely mutilated and perverted quotation. Neander says, in his "History of the Christian Religion and Church," Vol. I. pp. 571, 572 of Torrey's translation, which may be compared with pp. 984 – 986 of the original: —

"We now proceed to the doctrine in which Theism, taken in its connection with the proper and fundamental essence of Christianity, or with the doctrine of redemption, finds its ultimate completion, the *doctrine of the Trinity*. This doctrine *does not belong to the fundamental articles of the Christian faith;* [*] as appears

---

[*] I have omitted the word "strictly" which stands before "belong" in Torrey's translation of the first clause of this sentence, because it is an *interpolation* of the translator, to which

sufficiently evident from the fact, that it is expressly held forth in no one particular passage of the New Testament; for the only one in which this is done, the passage relating to the Three that bear record, (1 John v.,) is undoubtedly spurious, and in its ungenuine shape testifies to the fact, how foreign such a collocation is from the style of the New Testament Scriptures. We find in the New Testament no other fundamental article besides that of which the Apostle Paul says, that other foundation can no man lay than that is laid, the annunciation of Jesus as the Messiah; and Christ himself designates as the foundation of his religion, the faith in the only true God, and in Jesus Christ whom he hath sent. (John xvii. 3.) [More correctly, "in Jesus *the* Christ, *as* his Messenger," "*Jesus den Christ als seinen Gesandten.*"] What Paul styles distinctively the mystery, relates in no one instance to what belongs to the hidden depths of the divine essence, but to the divine purpose of salvation, which found its accomplishment in a fact. But that doctrine [i. e. the Trinity] presupposes, in order to its being understood in its real significancy for the Christian consciousness, this fundamental article of the Christian faith [i. e. the Messiahship of Jesus]; and we recognize therein the essential contents of Christianity, summed up in brief, as may be gathered from the determinate form which is given to Theism by its connection with this fundamental article. It is this doctrine by which God becomes known as the original

---

there is nothing corresponding in the original. Neander says, without any qualification, "*Diese Lehre gehört nicht zu den Grundartikeln des christlichen Glaubens.*" The English editor of Torrey's translation of Neander, the Rev. A. J. W. Morrison, who professes to have "carefully revised" it, instead of striking out the word "strictly," softens Neander's language still more. He makes the sentence read thus: — "This doctrine does not, *it appears to me*, belong *strictly* to the fundamental articles of the Christian faith," &c. (Vol. II. p. 286.)

Fountain of all existence; as he by whom the rational creation, that had become estranged from him, is brought back to the fellowship with him; and as he in the fellowship with whom it from thenceforth subsists: — the threefold relation in which God stands to mankind, as primal ground, mediator, and end, — Creator, Redeemer, Sanctifier, — in which threefold relation the whole Christian knowledge of God is completely announced. Accordingly, all is herein embraced [rather, "everything in this doctrine is brought together"] by the Apostle Paul, when he names the one God and Father of all, who is above all, and works through all and in all (Eph. iv. 6); or Him from whom are all things, through whom are all things, and to whom are all things; when, in pronouncing the benediction, he sums up all in the formula: the grace of the Lord Jesus Christ, the love of God, and the communion of the Holy Spirit. God, as the living God, the God of mankind, and the God of the Church, can be truly known in this way only."

On the next page, Neander distinguishes "the practical" doctrine of the Trinity, of which he is here speaking, — "which starts from God revealed in Christ, or from the position of the Apostle Paul, that God was in Christ reconciling the world to himself," — from "the speculative or ontological view." Of the former he says: "It is that which forms the basis of the true unity of the Church and the identity of the Christian consciousness in all ages. But the intellectual process of development, by means of which the economico-practical doctrine of the Trinity was reduced to the ontological, was a gradual one, and must necessarily run through manifold opposite forms."

In further illustration of the views of Neander, I quote from his " History of the Planting and Training of the Christian Church by the Apostles," as translated by Ryland, Vol. II. pp. 56, 57, Bohn's ed. He there says: —

"Both John and Paul place the essence of Christian theism in worshipping God as the Father, through the Son, in the communion of the divine life which he has established, or in the communion of the Holy Spirit, the Father through the Son dwelling in mankind animated by his Spirit, agreeably to the triad of the Pauline benediction, — the love of God, the grace of Christ, and the communion of the Holy Spirit (2 Cor. xiii. 13); and this is the basis of the doctrine of the Trinity in the connection of Christian experience. It has an essentially practical and historical significance and foundation; it is the doctrine of God revealed in humanity, which teaches men to recognize in God not only the original source of existence, but also of salvation and sanctification. From this trinity of revelation, as far as the divine causality images itself in the same, the reflective mind, according to the analogy of its own being, pursuing this track, seeks to elevate itself to the idea of an original triad in God, availing itself of the intimations which are contained in John's doctrine of the Logos, and the cognate elements of the Pauline theology."

It cannot be necessary to point out the difference between the common doctrine of the Trinity, which Dr. Huntington maintains, and that view of the Trinity, if we choose to adopt the name, which Neander presents as constituting it a *practical* doctrine. In the latter, it will be perceived, there is *nothing to which a Unitarian will not cordially assent.* But when, leaving this practical view of the Father, Son, and Holy Spirit, the "trinity of revelation," as Neander calls it, "the reflective mind seeks to elevate itself to the idea of an *origi-*

nal triad in God," and ventures to speculate on the mode of the divine existence, on " persons," or " hypostases," or " subsistences" in the nature of the One Infinite and Eternal Being, it

"Finds no end, in wandering mazes lost."

The result may be plain self-contradiction, as in the so-called Athanasian creed; it may be such expositions of "the Identity," "the Ipseity," "the Alterity," and "the Community," as are given us by Coleridge;* or such an elucidation of the mystery as Dr. Huntington (pp. 373, 374) quotes from Olshausen, who tells us that "*the knowledge which God possesses of himself is designated as the Son;* in him dwells the Father himself, and through him effects everything that he does effect. But as all the powers of the Father concentrate themselves, as it were, in his self-consciousness, so do they also continually revert from the Son to their primary source, the Father, and *this return is designated as the Holy Ghost!*" It may be a hundred other combinations of words without meaning; or it may be, far worse than this, the gross and material views which we find in writers like Flavel, who describe minutely the "bargain" of the persons of the Trinity in the so-called "Covenant of Redemption," in language which expresses conceptions of the Divine Being degraded to the level of Paganism.†

How refreshing to turn from such "darkening of counsel by words without knowledge," to the sterling

---

* See his *Literary Remains*. Works, V. 18, 19, Amer. ed.
† See Flavel's *Fountain of Life*, Serm. III.

sense of Jeremy Taylor, as expressed in the following passage, quoted by Bushnell in the extract given by Dr. Huntington, p. 414:—

" He who goes about to speak of the mystery of the Trinity, and does it by words and names of man's invention, talking of essences and existences, hypostases and personalities, priority in coequalities, and unity in pluralities, may amuse himself and build a tabernacle in his head, and talk of something he knows not what; but the good man who *feels* the power of the Father, to whom the Son is become wisdom, sanctification, and righteousness, and in whose heart the Spirit is shed abroad, — this man, though he understands nothing of what is unintelligible, yet he alone truly understands the Christian doctrine of the Trinity." *

Amen! E. A.

---

* This is a *condensation* rather than an exact quotation by Bushnell of a passage in Taylor's famous sermon before the University of Dublin, entitled *Via Intelligentiæ*. See his Works, Lond. 1828, Vol. VI. pp. 402, 403.

II.

DR. HUNTINGTON'S QUOTATIONS FROM SCRIPTURE IN PROOF OF THE TRINITY.

Mr. Editor:— In the last number of the Register, as some of your readers may recollect, notice was taken of a singular misquotation of Neander in Dr. Huntington's recent volume of sermons, entitled "Christian Believing and Living." The mistake by which that eminent theologian was made to say the opposite of what he does say, can only be explained by supposing that the sentence in question was hastily glanced at, and that no attention was paid to the context. I allude to this now simply for the purpose of remarking, that Dr. Huntington, in his sermon on the Trinity in the volume referred to, has quoted *Scripture* in several instances in much the same way in which he has quoted Neander. I mean by this, that he has cited detached expressions and fragments of sentences torn from their connection, in a manner adapted to produce a very different impression on the mind of the reader from that which would be made if the passages thus mutilated were quoted more fully. This mode of quotation is the more to be regretted, as no references are made to the places from which the passages cited are taken, so that the reader may not always be able to turn to them immediately, and examine the context for himself.

In making these statements, I have no thought of charging the Professor of Christian Morals in the University at Cambridge with any conscious unfairness or intentional misrepresentation. But I wish to illustrate and protest against a false mode of quoting and arguing from Scripture, into which theological writers of all denominations are apt to fall, and against which we should all be on our guard, taking care neither to practise it ourselves, nor to be deceived by it in others.

In p. 366 of his recent volume of sermons, Dr. Huntington says: "For him who has 'all power in heaven and earth' to say, 'Of that day and hour knoweth not the Son,' is condescension indeed." In p. 527 he also says of Christ, "'All power' is his 'in heaven and earth.'" The passage referred to is Matt. xxviii. 18, where our Saviour says, "All power is *given* unto me in heaven and in earth." This little word "given" would not have greatly increased the length of the quotation.

Again (p. 366) he quotes as proof of our Saviour's deity the declaration, "He that hath seen me hath seen the Father." (John xiv. 9.) It was, perhaps, hardly to be expected that he should add the words of the next verse: "Believest thou not that I am in the Father and the Father in me? The words that I speak unto you I speak not of myself; but the Father that dwelleth in me he doeth the works."

Dr. Huntington continues his argument by saying: "Paul speaks of Christ as set 'far above all principality and power, and might and dominion, and every name that is named, not only in this world, but also in that which is to come.' Can this be a creature?"

The verse thus quoted is Eph. i. 21. It is part of a sentence, in which Paul is speaking of the work of God's mighty power, "which he wrought in Christ, when he *raised him* from the dead and *set him* at his own right hand in the heavenly places, far above all principality and power, and might and dominion, and every name that is named, not only in this world, but also in that which is to come; and *hath put all things under his feet*, and *gave* him to be the head over all things to the Church, which is his body, the fulness of him that filleth all in all."

Dr. Huntington proceeds to quote as follows: "That at the name of Jesus every knee should bow, and every tongue confess that he is Lord," adding the question, "Is not this a being to whom prayer is to be offered?"

The passage as thus quoted begins very abruptly with a "*that*," and is also shorn of its conclusion. The whole sentence reads as follows: "Wherefore God also *hath highly exalted* him, and *given* him a name that is above every name; that at the name of Jesus [literally, "*in* the name of Jesus"] every knee should bow, of things in heaven, and things in earth, and things under the earth; and that every tongue should confess that Jesus Christ is Lord, *to the glory of God, the Father*." (Phil. ii. 9 – 11.)

In p. 372 Dr. Huntington begins another quotation in the same way with a "*that*," — "That all men should honor the Son even as they honor the Father," &c. The whole sentence reads as follows: "For the Father judgeth no man, but hath *committed* all judgment unto the Son; that all men should honor the Son, even as they honor the Father. He that honoreth not the Son, honoreth not the Father which hath *sent* him." (John v. 22, 23.)

In the note to the same sermon, p. 525, there are instances in which Dr. Huntington detaches certain expressions from their connection, applying them to a subject to which they do not relate, or to which, at least, they are not expressly applied in the original. Thus, referring to Phil. ii. 7, 8, he says of our Saviour, "So he 'took on' the form of man. He 'humbled himself' to be human." The expressions of Paul are, "He took upon him *the form of a servant*,' — "he humbled himself, and *became obedient unto death*, even the death of the cross."

Again Dr. Huntington says (p. 525), "He 'left the glory he had with the Father before the world was.'" Here the word *left* is improperly put within quotation marks. The reference is to John xvii. 5, where eminent Trinitarian commentators have understood the glory which Christ *prays for*, "the glory which he had with the Father before the world was," to mean the glory which was *destined* for him as the Messiah in the eternal purpose of God.

On p. 527 we find an extraordinary misquotation and misapprehension of an important passage. Dr. Huntington is here treating of prayer to Christ, which he calls "a richer worship" (p. 528) than prayer to the Father. Speaking of our Saviour's discourse at the Last Supper, he remarks : —

" He said, too, speaking of the sad, impending hour of separation, when he foresaw that the hearts and minds of his followers would be torn with anguish and doubt, half paralyzed by fear, and alternating between fond remembrances of his bodily appearance and new thoughts of the spiritual relation to subsist thenceforth between them, — ' *In that hour* ye shall (or will) ask me nothing.'

But he adds, very considerately, to console them, Nevertheless, your halting faith shall not forfeit the blessing. 'Whatsoever ye shall ask the Father, *in my name*, he will give it you;' and again, 'If ye shall ask anything in my name, *I will do it.*' The whole passage evidently relates to the distinction between his outward and his eternal presence, between the visible and the invisible intercourse of his followers with him. In a remoter and calmer period his worship would take its place spontaneously in their hymns, ejaculations, and litanies. Meantime, he points them to the Father in whom they are already believing with a more settled and definite faith."

The verse which Dr. Huntington thus quotes and explains, is John xvi. 23. Asking the reader to turn to it, I will quote it in connection with the preceding and the following verse, which will be sufficient to show how utterly he has mistaken its meaning. Our Saviour says to his disciples:—

" And ye now therefore have sorrow. But I will see you again, and your heart shall rejoice, and your joy no man taketh from you. And in that day ye shall ask me nothing. Verily, verily, I say unto you, Whatsoever ye shall ask the Father in my name, he will give it you. Hitherto ye have asked nothing in my name; ask, and ye shall receive, that your joy may be full."

By the expression " in that day," Dr. Huntington understands " the sad, impending hour of separation, when the hearts and minds of Christ's followers would be torn with anguish and doubt," when, on account of their " halting faith," they would not have confidence to address their prayers directly to him, as they would " in a remoter and calmer period;" and in accordance with this view, in quoting the passage, he takes the liberty to substitute "*hour*" for "*day*." But how evident it is, that the meaning is just the reverse; that the expression refers to the time after his resurrection, when he would "see them again" and be with them again in spirit, and "their hearts would rejoice," with a joy which no human power could destroy. He is speaking of the time when the Holy Spirit would enlighten their minds and comfort their hearts, guiding them into such a knowledge of the truth as they could not attain while he was with them in the flesh. The expression "in that day" is used as it is in the 26th verse of the same chapter, and in John xiv. 20, which, with its context, should be compared with the present passage. I am not aware that any commentator, in any age, ever dreamt of understanding this passage in the way in which it is explained by Dr. Huntington.

It is proper, however, to remark, that the word "ask," in the first clause of the 23d verse, is ambiguous. It may mean either "to ask a question," or "to ask a favor," "to request." John often uses it in both senses. It is a different word in the original from that translated "ask" in the last part of the verse. The sentence, "In that day ye shall (or will) ask me nothing," has been understood by many to mean, "At that time you will have no need to question me." The doubts which now perplex you will be removed. But whether this is the true meaning or not, the fact is incontrovertible, that our Saviour uniformly directed his disciples to address their prayers, not to himself, nor to the Holy Spirit, as a distinct person in the Trinity, but to the Father in his name.

I will give another specimen of Dr. Huntington's expositions of Scripture. He says (p. 367):—

"At last ..... this incarnate 'Head over all things to the Church' will render up the kingdom to the Father, and resume his place in the coequal Three, the indivisible One. Mark the expressions. (1 Cor. xv. 24, 28.) It is the Son who hath put 'all things under his feet,' 'all rule, authority, and power,' who is 'subject unto God ($\upsilon\pi o\tau\alpha\gamma\eta\sigma\epsilon\tau\alpha\iota$, 'arranged under'). Just after, it is God that 'hath put all things under him.' In this sense, therefore, God and the Son are the same, for the same mastery is asserted of each. But the Son, in his character of Sonship, is retaken, so to speak, into the everlasting, almighty, ineffable, undivided One, where the distinctions of office which had aided us so greatly in apprehending the glorious Trinity are lost to our sight. It is not anything peculiar to one of the Three Persons, but God in whom they all are One, who then 'is all in all.'"

Such is the comment. The following is the text:—

"Then cometh the end, when he shall have delivered up the kingdom to God, even the Father: when he shall have put down all rule and all authority and power. For he must reign, till he hath put all enemies under his feet. The last enemy that shall be destroyed is Death. For he [i. e. God] hath put all things under his feet. (Ps. viii. 6.) But when he saith, All things are put under him, it is manifest that He is excepted, which did put all things under him. And when all things shall be subdued unto him, THEN *shall the Son also himself be subject unto him that put all things under him,* that God may be all in all."

In p. 363, Dr. Huntington quotes the expression "God manifest in the flesh," as if it were a scriptural designation of Christ. The reference is to 1 Tim. iii. 16. The expression itself is one which a Unitarian might very naturally use, to represent more vividly the fact that "God was in Christ, reconciling the world unto himself;" but if quoted as an argument for the doctrine of the deity of Christ, it should be understood that the leading Trinitarian critics of the present day, on the authority of the best manuscripts and early versions, regard the word "God," in the passage referred to, as a corruption of the original text, the true reading being not Θεός, "God," but ὅς, "who," or "he who." Such is the view of Olshausen, Meyer, De Wette, Wiesinger, Huther, Bunsen, Davidson, Green, Jowett, and the recent editors Lachmann, Tischendorf, Tregelles, Alford, Ellicott, and Wordsworth, to say nothing of Griesbach, and others among the older critics. E. A.

III.

DR. HUNTINGTON AND DR. POND.

DR. HUNTINGTON has found his way to a belief in a Trinity through what he conceives to be the "needs, the longings" of the soul. The suffering of any nature lower than the Divine does not meet the grand want of man. "It is only as we find . . . . . the nameless and inexpressible anguish of a Divine and Infinite Being . . . . . that the signals of the Passion are lifted into any genuine honor." "Without this, they . . . . . fail even of respect." . . . . . "When the Saviour suffered, God suffered." "When the mortal part of the Saviour died, God suffered with him." "And in that dying . . . . . there was involved God's anguish for his sinning children." "Now this is precisely what an inferior faith fails to gain. Raise your conception of Christ's rank in the scale of created being as high as you may . . . . . both practically and logically the needed atonement fails. God himself is not in the suffering. This [i. e. that God should suffer] was the requirement of the case. This was the longing of the guilty heart. This is what the Gospel, from end to end, in plain, and full, and glorious language declares."

Such is Dr. Huntington's declaration of the need of human nature; there must be a Trinity; and God, nor simply human nature, or the human nature in which the Son was incarnated, must have suffered for sin. This is all very clear and very explicit. The only question about it is whether it is true. If I were to bring my view of human need as an offset to his, Dr. Huntington would probably say that I was not a proper judge in such a case, that Unitarian experience was not "deep" enough nor "searching" enough to enable one to speak of the "profound" needs of the soul. So it would be a waste of time for me to attempt a denial of the asserted need, and furnished supply. So I will stand aside and introduce the Rev. Enoch Pond, D. D., Professor of Theology in Bangor Theological Seminary, a man of advanced age, of most thorough and undisputed Orthodoxy during all his years, doubtless sinner enough to have some correct conceptions of a sinner's needs, and a sufficiently thorough student of the Bible to know what it says about the supply of them. What says the old veteran theologian whose long life has been spent in the light of Orthodox theology, and who ought to know something about it? In the "Bibliotheca Sacra and Theological Review" for April, 1850, the venerable Professor has discussed this very point, which has so exercised the mind and heart of Dr. Huntington, and has given us at great length, and with great store of learning and severity of logic, his view of the subject. Let us hear the declaration of this oracle of Trinitarianism. "Did he [Christ] suffer only as a man, a divinely strengthened and supported man; or did the Divinity also suffer?" This is the question answered. "Did God as well as man suffer?" This is the question Dr. Pond discusses, and he answers it peremptorily in the negative; flatly contradicts Dr. Huntington, and emphatically denies the only view of Christ's sufferings which can "satisfy the longings of the guilty heart." Through two pages the venerable Professor of Bangor quotes passages to show that it is utterly unscriptural to assert that the Divine nature in Christ suffered. He says that they prove "as certainly as words can prove anything, that our Saviour's sufferings (if we except those of mere sympathy) were confined to his human nature." Dr. Pond says the Bible is against Dr. Huntington's view. We shall therefore wait and see if the Bangor veteran follows the new light before we run after it. Till then we shall rest quietly in our Unitarianism, and believe that the Scriptures teach that human nature only suffered on the cross, and also continue to believe that such a view of our Saviour's sufferings is sufficient for all the needs of any "guilty heart."

But Dr. Pond goes further. He says that to suppose our Saviour's suffering "extended to the Divine nature, to God, is inconsistent with his *acknowledged perfections.*" "What possible idea," he exclaims, "can we frame of these sufferings if we say that they were the sufferings of God himself?" "Who can conceive of such a thing? Who can contemplate it but with distress and horror?" Dr. Pond's idea of what the "guilty heart" requires differs very widely from Dr. Huntington's. "Distress and horror" fill the heart of the venerable Professor of Bangor as he contemplates the only doctrine which the Plummer Professor at Cambridge says can give peace and trust to the sinner. Surely, when such discordant voices are uttered, one may well be pardoned for waiting till the infallible guides are agreed, before he deserts the old path of Channing and Ware.

After describing still further the "logical" absurdities of the view that "God suffered," Dr. Pond says, "If these expressions shall seem to any of my readers irreverent and awful, I cannot help it. They are no more irreverent than the theory which I am laboring to expose." So Dr. Pond pronounces Dr. Huntington's theory, to embrace which he felt compelled to abandon the Unitarians, "*irreverent*"!! Surely there is something new under the sun; a good man leaves the heresies of his old associates, and his associates also, and rushes among the ranks of their opposers, flaunting in the faces of his new friends the declaration of his faith, which ten years before had been pronounced by one of the veteran commanders of the hosts of God's elect, "*irreverent*," "*demonstrably false*"!! It is said that a great statesman once asked despondingly, "Where shall *I* go?" After a few pages more, in which the absurdity of the Divine sufferings is illustrated, Dr. Pond says,

"I here close my argument against this *strange*, and to my apprehension, *monstrous* idea, that the Divine nature of Christ participated directly in the sufferings of the cross." The Italics are mine.

Dr. Huntington is confident, respecting the doctrine of the Trinity, that the heart of all Christendom could not have been in an error for so many ages. Dr. Pond says that the doctrine of the suffering of the Divine nature is a new one; has come up within a few years; was almost universally rejected for eighteen centuries. Now if the almost universal *belief* of the Church for eighteen hundred years is good evidence of the truth of the doctrine of the Trinity, it would seem to be equally good proof of the erroneousness of Dr. Huntington's view of the longings of the guilty heart, and their satisfaction by the sufferings of the Divine nature, that all these ages *rejected* his doctrine. At least I think so. Dr. Pond confutes Dr. Huntington.

The Bangorian Professor has a "horror" of the results of Dr. Huntington's doctrine. He says its fruits "will be bitter, like all the products of delusion and error." It is positively too bad to have this grave Down-easter meet the jubilant neophyte, who has just discovered the *only* doctrine which will satisfy the "longing of the guilty heart," with a flat affirmation that it is mere "delusion and error." Evangelicism is a queer thing. Dr. Pond says further, that the tendency of this doctrine "will be to degrade and dishonor him [God]." It will be no comfort to the Plummer Professor to be told that his Bangor brother says, "The views I have controverted, should they extensively prevail, will be likely to drive many into simple Unitarianism." More and worse. "The doctrine of a suffering Deity, of a crucified God, is TOO REVOLTING [these capitals are ours] to obtain currency with THINKING minds, [that is too bad, Dr. Pond;] and, if this shall come to be insisted on as essential to Orthodoxy, not a few will renounce it altogether. It will lead 'persons' to reject the atonement altogether, and trust to the work of their own hands for salvation." "It is always safe to follow the Bible, honestly, faithfully, reasonably interpreted; but specious theories and startling novelties are to be suspected and avoided."

But enough, enough. I have shown that one of the most venerable and eminent evangelical theologians pronounced, ten years ago, the view which gives Dr. Huntington so much joy, and which alone can "satisfy the longings of the guilty heart," a "delusion and error," "contrary to Scripture," "inconsistent with God's acknowledged perfection," "too revolting to obtain currency with thinking minds," and "likely [most awful of all] to drive many into simple Unitarianism"!!

R. P. S.

IV.

LETTER FROM PROF. HUNTINGTON.

Cambridge, Jan. 30, 1860.

Mr. Reed:—Your correspondent, "E. A.," charges me with a misquotation from Neander, in a sermon on the Trinity. The explanation is simple, but not wholly satisfactory even to myself. The quotation was transferred from an article by a theological writer, whose accuracy I had no reason to question, and whose honesty is above suspicion, where many of the readers of the "Register" must have seen it. Knowing Neander, as every one familiar with his various writings knows him, to be a Trinitarian, I did not verify the extract by a reference to the author. I trust I have no pride to prevent my saying that it would have been better if I had. It would have saved me some reproach and your correspondent some trouble. The citation makes Neander say that the doctrine of the Trinity is "the fundamental article of the Christian faith, the essential contents of Christianity summed up in brief." The first clause should be omitted. It appears that Neander, in that passage of his history, makes a distinction between "fundamental" and "essential," a distinction of which the sincere disbeliever in the doctrine ought to have the full advantage. I suppose my authority was misled by the language of the context, where the Messiahship of Christ is spoken of as the "fundamental" doctrine. Had my very near neighbor, my fellow-officer in College, whose daily walks cross mine, whom I saw in your office at the very moment when he was probably arranging for the publication of his article, intimated to me his surprise, I might have relieved him in a word, and would willingly have published the correction. But perhaps this would not have served the purpose.

Now, as to what sort of a Trinitarian Neander was. This is a matter of very little importance to my sermon, but " E. A." has undertaken an exposition of it which deserves a moment's attention. He asserts that according to Neander, "the doctrine of the Trinity *includes* the essential elements of Christianity, as husks include the ear, or as wheat may be included in a collection of chaff." Fortunately, there is the less need to restate or interpret the great historian's opinions, as he has set them forth distinctly enough in more than one of his productions, some of which are translated into our language and are commonly accessible. Whoever is interested in this question will do well, having marked the representation just given, to turn to those passages of the "History," easily found by the ample index in each volume, where the doctrine is discussed in connection with the successive periods of the doctrinal development of the Church; and also to corresponding passages in the "History of Christian Dogmas," in two volumes (Bohn) edited by Dr. Jacobi, and translated by Ryland, especially to the sections (Vol. II. pp. 645 – 650) treating of the belief as unfolded in the third principal Period. It will very soon appear *how* he distinguishes between all heresies on this subject and the true faith of the Church. He not only affirms that "the essence of all Christianity is contained in it," but that the doctrine of the Trinity is "the *perfect development of the doctrine about Christ;*" and "that it is *rooted in the centre-point of Christianity.*" In the "*Life of Christ*" he says, "Christ does not refuse the title given to him by Thomas; he acknowledges his exclamation ('My Lord and my God!') as an expression of the true faith." In the paragraph after that one from which "E. A." chiefly quotes, Neander asserts the "connection" of the doctrine of the Trinity with "the *fundamental consciousness of Christianity*." In the next following occur several sentences which we prefer to give entire, rather than in "E. A.'s" somewhat fragmentary representations: "Only we are not to forget that the practical or economical Triad, which starts from God revealed in Christ, or from the position of the Apostle Paul, that God was in Christ, reconciling the world to Himself, must ever be considered as the *groundwork of the whole*, the original element from which the speculative, or ontological, view is derived; a position which we shall find substantiated in tracing, as we now propose to do, the historical development of this doctrine in these first centuries. This economico-practical doctrine of the Trinity *constituted from the beginning the fundamental consciousness of the Catholic Church*, while forming itself in its conflict with the opposite theories of the heretical sects. It is that which forms the basis of the true unity of the Church, and the identity of the Christian consciousness in all ages." The next sentence, as rendered by Torrey, "E. A.," who advocates complete quotations and dislikes "mutilation," cuts in two, stopping short with the word "forms." "But the intellectual process of development, by means of which the economico-practical doctrine of the Trinity was reduced to the ontological, was a gradual one, and must necessarily run through manifold opposite forms, *until it issued at last in some mode of apprehension, satisfying the demand of unity in the Christian consciousness and in the activity of the dialectic reason.*" These words conclude a paragraph, and they have a bearing on the historical argument.

Again, speaking of the establishment of the Feast of the Holy Trinity, after contrasting it with the Feast of the Virgin, and observing that it has not, like many festivals, a date from any special historical fact or incident, Neander goes on thus: —

"Yet if there was something in the Christian consciousness that resisted the introduction of a festival of the Immaculate Conception of Mary, there was, on the other hand, an appropriateness in a festival of the Trinity, constituting, as it were, a sort of terminus to the entire cycle of festivals in the year, which would recommend it to general acceptance, and gradually overcome the objections which might be raised on the ground of innovation. For it corresponded with the relation of the doctrine of the Trinity to the sum total of Christian consciousness, that as this doctrine has for its presupposition the full development of all that is contained in this consciousness, *the Christian consciousness arrives therein at a statement which exhausts the whole subject-matter:* so a festival having reference to this doctrine would form the terminus of the cycle of festivals, commencing with Christ's nativity; and if this festival grew in the first place out of the significance which the doctrine of the Trinity has gained for the speculative and mystical theology of these times, yet this solemnity obtained a position which was calculated to direct attention to the original and essential significance of this doctrine."

Whether, in view of this language, especially of that printed in Italics, the remarks that Neander makes "the doctrine of the Trinity to include the essential elements of Christianity as husks include the ear or as wheat may be included in a collection of chaff," can be considered as a very successful or happy reproduction of Neander's idea, may be judged by the readers of both. If, as I understand "E. A." to state, there is "nothing" in that idea "to which a Unitarian will not cordially assent," I have only to say it is the best of all recent intelligence. That there is some agreement, though on terms of vast inequality, between the main drift of my sermon and Neader's practical handling of the same theme, in carefully separating the spiritual import from the "dialectic theories," though a theory is given — is what I should have ventured to suppose, and what most of those who have noticed my sermon have suggested. But of this I have no right to be confident.

Neander's historical judgment, expressed in the last quoted passage but one, and sustained through his great work, will probably present itself as some offset in point of authority, to the assertion of those who say that the Trinity was unknown to the early Christian centuries.

In another article, "E. A." has pointed out several instances in which I have so omitted the context, in Scriptural quotations, as to leave out of sight language that ascribes dependence, subjection, etc., to the person of Jesus in the mediatorial office. I believe I have explicitly and repeatedly admitted in my sermon the existence and natural force of that whole class of texts; nay, have recognized them as indispensable to the truth, and most precious to the believer. It was not pertinent to my object to copy them, while I was striving to bring out especially the other side of the twofold whole, any more than it would be the *Register's* object to copy and commend much of those four fifths of my volume to which it probably consents. But to expect to conceal them from the reader's knowledge, or to wish to do it, would imply a presumption or a falsity which I know my good friend would not impute to me. All other matters of difference between us I cheerfully submit to the public, and to the Master.

In another quarter I have been alleged, it is said, to have made a wrong quotation from St. Paul, because I have *translated* the original word (κοινωνία), in one of the Apostle's benedictions, by our word "fellowship," whereas the common version has it "communion;" giving rise to a humorous intimation that I am joined to an indefinite company of blunderers who have mistaken the Book of Common Prayer for the Bible. But when it is remembered that the same Greek word has "fellowship" for a legitimate meaning, and is actually translated "fellowship" in Acts ii. 42, 1 Cor. i. 9, 2 Cor. viii. 4, Gal. ii. 9, and Phil. i. 5. I apprehend that scholars, and all such as happen to know that St. Paul did not write to the Corinthians in English, will acquit me on this count.

Whether these particulars really affect the general force of the train of thought offered in the discourse, or whether that force, be it less or more, would be much weakened if all these particulars were otherwise, I must refer to the candid decision of minds more impartial than I can pretend to be.

Forbear with me if I beg further for space to appeal briefly to the nobler and more reverential moods of another of your correspondents, "R. P. S." Why seek to throw odium on any sincere student, or conviction, by such phrases as "new light," "infallible guides," "flaunting in the faces of his new friends the declaration of his faith," "the jubilant neophyte"? I want to say to all this, — My brother! What better thing can we do for one another, in this life of so much darkness and weakness, than report earnestly to one another what we see or honestly think we see, and tell out any joy we have found? "We can do nothing against the truth, but for the truth." If our joy is unfounded, it will be taken from us soon enough. If it is excessive, there are sorrows enough to weigh it down. One of these with me, is that I am made by my faith to be a cause of offence to many whom I esteem and love, — R. P. S. among them. If, as I confess to be possible, I have added to the inevitable provocation by any harshness or bitterness, it has been against a steady effort to the contrary; and I beg forgiveness of all that feel aggrieved. I am sure I never felt it so easy to be charitable to all men as now. Would to God these friends could so see the revelation of God's Tri-unity in all its real and profound relations, that it would cease to be a vital interest, whether for speculation or for sarcasm, what exposition different theologians may give of the *mode* in which the doctrine is to be held or applied! Enough that the redeeming and consoling result is reached and held, and by each in his own way. Would to God we all could have the light and power of this belief so borne in upon our souls that the ruling desire should be, not to defend a party, but to communicate the gracious gift, and to behold others glad and strong in it! Meantime it is not too late to recall those days of "Channing and Ware," of Greenwood and Norton and Nichols, when themes so high and holy were touched with soberness, dignity, and awe, when an elevated culture forbade all flippancy and levity, when pulpit personalities were unknown, and when opponents did not court the advantage of one another's violations of patience or self-respect. Not ready to cast the first stone, I am yours, not without regret for the past, but with hope for the future, and with unfailing regard for yourself.

F. D. H.

V.

REVIEW OF DR. HUNTINGTON'S LETTER.

Mr. Editor:— I greatly regret the necessity of taking any notice of Dr. Huntington's communication in the last number of the Register. I have no taste for newspaper controversy; and in the two articles to which Dr. Huntington refers, it was my purpose to quote him, and Neander, and the New Testament, so fully and fairly, that he should have no ground of complaint, and that there should be no need of a rejoinder, if a reply were made. Nothing has, in fact, been said or quoted by Dr. Huntington, which in the slightest degree invalidates any statement I have there made; but through some strange misapprehension, he has ascribed to me certain extraordinary statements which I have *not* made. In refuting these imaginary statements, he is triumphantly successful. He proves conclusively that Neander was a Trinitarian; a fact which I took care to mention near the beginning of my article.

Allow me, then, Mr. Editor, to state clearly what I am charged with saying, and what I actually did say.

I am sorry, indeed, to be thus compelled to ask the attention of your readers to a matter in itself of so little consequence; but it will afford an opportunity, perhaps, for the illustration of something more important.

Speaking of the question, — which, however, I did not raise or discuss, — " as to what sort of a Trinitarian Neander was," Dr. Huntington says, "' E. A.' has undertaken an exposition of it which deserves a moment's attention. He asserts *that according to Neander*, [the Italics are mine] 'the doctrine of the Trinity *includes* the essential elements of Christianity, as husks include the ear, or as wheat may be included in a collection of chaff.'" He again ascribes to me "the remark *that Neander makes* 'the doctrine of the Trinity to include the essential elements of Christianity as husks include the ear,'" &c. He further "understands 'E. A.' to state, that there is 'nothing' in Neander's idea [of the Trinity] 'to which a Unitarian will not cordially assent.'"

What I said was this: —

[Here E. A. quotes the principal part of the second paragraph of his first article, to which the reader is requested to turn. See pp. 162, 163.]

What ground, now, could Dr. Huntington have imagined himself to have for asserting that I represented *Neander* as making the doctrine of the Trinity include the essential elements of Christianity as husks include the ear, &c.? Have I ascribed any such language to him? Please look again at the words in question. In what way could I have contrived more clearly to express the sentiment as *my own*, and not another's?

A very few words on another point. I am sorry that

Dr. Huntington should have thought it necessary to introduce personal matters into his communication, the more so as he labors under a misapprehension in regard to one of the principal facts. At the time to which he refers, my whole article was in type. It had been given to the publisher of the Register just a week before. So far as Dr. Huntington is personally concerned, it would have been more agreeable to me to have pointed out his mistake to him privately, and to have allowed him to correct it in his own way. But it appeared to me that it would promote the cause of Christian truth and charity to show by large quotations the contrast between his view of the *importance* of the doctrine of the Trinity and that of Neander. *This* Dr. Huntington could hardly have been expected to do. I therefore chose to make the correction a public one. I would, however, now respectfully suggest to Dr. Huntington, that as the Register will probably reach a very small proportion of the readers of his sermons, it may be well for him to make the correction in some Orthodox newspaper of extensive circulation, as, for example, the New York Independent.

I regret, however, to observe, that our friend has not got his quotation exactly right yet. He had ascribed to Neander the statement, that "the doctrine of the Trinity is the fundamental article of the Christian faith, — the essential contents of Christianity summed up in brief." Now he says: —

"The first clause should be omitted. It appears that Neander, in that passage of his history, makes a distinction between 'fundamental' and 'essential,' a distinction of which the sincere disbeliever in the doctrine ought to have the full advantage."

Here Dr. Huntington, I conceive, misunderstands Neander. I know of no intelligible distinction, which is not either merely arbitrary or etymological, between the meaning of the terms "fundamental" and "essential," as applied to Christian doctrines. Neander makes no such distinction as Dr. Huntington imagines. He does *not* say, as I am very sorry to be compelled to repeat, that "the doctrine of the Trinity *is* the essential contents of Christianity, summed up in brief." That would be the same as calling it fundamental. He says that "that doctrine *presupposes*, in order to its being understood in its real significance for the Christian consciousness," that is, in order that it may have any practical value, "the fundamental article of the Christian faith," namely, the Messiahship of Jesus: and that accordingly "we recognize *in* it the essential contents of Christianity, summed up in brief." I do not deem it necessary to give any new illustration of the distinction between what a thing *is* and what is *contained in* it." The expression which Neander uses, "we recognize therein," taken by itself, may admit of the sense which Dr. Huntington gives it; but it certainly does not require this interpretation. On the contrary, to give it this meaning here, is to make Neander contradict what he has just said.

Neander's style is not remarkable for clearness; his sentences are sometimes long and involved, and even ungrammatical; and his mode of thought is peculiarly German. Still, his general meaning can seldom be mistaken by an attentive reader. In my former article, I avoided, as far as possible, stating his views in my own language, and left him, by ample quotations, to speak for himself. Requesting the reader who takes an interest in the matter to recur to those quotations, I propose to give some additional illustrations of the broad distinction between what he calls "the practical," or "economico-practical doctrine of the Trinity," "which constituted from the beginning the fundamental consciousness of the Catholic Church," and "the speculative or ontological" doctrine. The latter is the doctrine of the Trinity as it appears in most of the creeds of the Church, and in that of Dr. Huntington; it is characterized by the fact, that it undertakes to define the mode of the divine existence, and to point out the mutual relations of the "persons," as it calls them, in the Godhead. (In connection with this, it assumes also to define the *mode* in which God was united with the man Jesus Christ.) In the form in which Dr. Huntington receives it, for example, it teaches that in the unity of the Godhead there are three "coequal persons," each God, and all but one God, to each of whom divine worship is to be offered, the worship of the Son, however, being a "richer worship" than that of the Father; it speaks of the eternal generation of the Son from the Father, and of the eternal procession of the Holy Spirit from both.

In this and in the other forms in which it appears in creeds, it is to be observed that this doctrine is not only not expressly taught in any passage of Scripture, but that it does not admit of being stated in Scripture language. It is, confessedly, wholly a doctrine of *inference*.

On the other hand, "the *practical* doctrine of the Trinity" does not, as Neander explains it, meddle with the question of the mode of the divine existence; it says nothing of three coequal, coeternal persons in the Godhead, each of whom is a distinct object of worship. It is concerned only with the relations of God to man. It recognizes God, the Creator and Ruler of all things, as having revealed himself in and through Jesus Christ, as the merciful Father of men, the God of love; and as communicating spiritual light and life, joy and strength, to every believing soul, by his Holy Spirit. It also recognizes the fact that God was so united with Christ that he speaks to us with divine authority; and that in him we behold, as Neander expresses it, "the perfect man as the image of the perfect God." In him the divine and human were morally blended into one.

As Dr. Huntington has perverted the meaning of one of my sentences by applying it to a subject to which I did not apply it, I will repeat a part of the extract given in my former article, from Neander's "Planting and Training," &c., II. 56, Bohn's ed. Neander there says:—

"Both John and Paul place the essence of Christian theism in worshipping God as the Father, through the Son, in the communion of the divine life which he has established, or in the communion of the Holy Spirit; ..... and this is the basis of the doctrine of the Trinity in the connection of Christian experience. It has an essentially practical and historical significance and foundation: it is the doctrine of God revealed in humanity, which teaches men to recognize in God not only the original source of existence, but also of salvation and sanctification."

On the view of the Trinity which Neander *here presents* as constituting it a *practical* doctrine, I remarked that "there is nothing in it to which a Unitarian will not cordially assent." Is not this plainly so? Is not the *worship* described in the first sentence Unitarian, and a very different thing from worshipping the Father, *and* the Son, *and* the Holy Spirit, as distinct persons in a Trinity? Again, do not all Unitarians recognize in God "not only the original source of existence, but also of salvation and sanctification?"

That Neander himself rested in this simple, practical view, I have never said, or implied, but the contrary. In the sentence which follows, and which I quoted in my previous article, he goes on to speak of the speculative view, implying, as I understood it, his own reception of the doctrine of "an original triad in God." But Dr. Huntington "understands 'E. A.' to state that there is 'nothing' in *Neander's* idea [i. e. of the *Trinity*, which the context requires the reader to supply] 'to which a Unitarian will not cordially assent.'" Here, as elsewhere in his article, all that gives the slightest appearance of plausibility to his criticisms, is his complete misunderstanding and consequent perversion of what I actually said.

The length of this article has so far exceeded reasonable limits, that I must omit much which I wished to say and to quote. But I will give the introductory paragraph of Neander's remarks on the doctrine of the Trinity in his "History of Christian Dogmas," Bohn's ed., Vol. I. p. 130. He says:—

"In reference to the historical development of this doctrine, we must distinguish between its practical or economical importance, and its speculative construction. Its practical, Christian value is closely connected with the doctrine of Jesus the Redeemer, and presents the threefold distinction of Christian Theism, the doctrine of one God as the Creator and Father of men, who has revealed himself in Christ, — of the Son of God through whom he has revealed himself, — and of the source of divine life which has been conveyed from the Son to the human race. This doctrine of God, the Creator, Redeemer, and Sanctifier of humanity in Christ was essential to the Christian consciousness, and therefore has existed from the beginning in the Christian Church. (Compare 2 Cor. xiii. 13, Rom. xi. 36.) In the various recensions of the Apostles' Creed it is announced as the peculiar article of Christian faith in opposition to Judaism and Paganism, and has been received by the whole Church. [Here I remark that everybody knows that the Apostles' Creed, so called, is purely Unitarian.] But *the intellectual construction of this doctrine is something different*, and *was not fixed till a later period* in that definite, dogmatic form of expression which now prevails. We have to treat of the manner in which the relation of the Trinity to Unity was determined, — of the speculative construction of the doctrine of God's being in Christ, and of the Holy Spirit in connection with the Unity of the Divine Being."

In the second volume of his Church History, as translated by Torrey, p. 348, note, Neander observes that, among the subjects which Gregory Nazianzen (in the latter half of the fourth century) speaks of as discussed in the public teaching of those times,

"he names as the principal thing the doctrine of the Trinity, although this doctrine surely derives its *Christian* importance only from its connection with that doctrine which Gregory represents as a subordinate one [the doctrine of redemption]; although entire Christianity starts not from a speculative doctrine concerning the Divine Being, but from the actual revelation of God, as a fact in history."

Dr. Huntington quotes a sentence from Neander, which I gave only in part, and intimates that I have exposed myself to the charge of "mutilation." I am glad he has quoted it fully, as every reader must perceive that no injustice was done to Neander by the omission, and that I could have had no motive for omitting it, except to save room. It has, as Dr. Huntington remarks, "a bearing on the historical argument," a subject into which I did not pretend to enter. But its bearing, the reader will notice, is directly *against* Dr. Huntington's assumption, that the doctrine of the Trinity has been received in the Christian Church in all ages. This is a point which I should be very glad to illustrate; but I have already, Mr. Editor, occupied far too much of your space.

With respect to Dr. Huntington's mode of quoting Scripture, of which examples were given in the Register for January 28, I only wish to call the attention of your readers to the fact, that he defends it as proper.

E. A.

VI.

GRADUAL DEVELOPMENT OF THE DOCTRINE OF THE TRINITY.

Mr. Editor : — In former articles, I have illustrated the distinction which Neander so often makes between what he calls "the practical" or "economical" doctrine of the Trinity, and "the speculative or ontological view." The former he regards as "the groundwork" of the latter, "the original element from which it is derived." It "starts from God revealed in Christ, or from the doctrine of the Apostle Paul, that God was in Christ reconciling the world to himself." It has nothing to do with any distinctions in the divine nature. We recognize in it, according to Neander, simply "the threefold *relation* in which God stands to mankind, as primal ground, mediator, and end, — Creator, Redeemer, and Sanctifier, — in which threefold relation the *whole Christian knowledge of God is completely announced.*" It is, in fact, all involved in the doctrine of the Messiahship of Jesus, which, as Neander everywhere maintains, is the only essential article of the Christian faith. In this "practical doctrine of the Trinity," I again repeat, there are no elements which do not belong to pure Unitarianism. And it is "this economico-practical doctrine of the Trinity" — not the doctrine of three co-equal persons in one God, not *any* doctrine about the mode of the divine existence — which, according to Neander,

"constituted from the beginning the fundamental consciousness of the Catholic Church, while [this Church was] forming itself in its conflict with the opposite theories of the heretical sects. It is that which forms the basis of the true unity of the Church and the identity of the Christian consciousness in all ages. But the intellectual process of development, by means of which the economico-practical doctrine of the Trinity was *reduced to the ontological*, was a *gradual* one, and must necessarily *run through manifold opposite forms*, until it issued *at last* in some mode of apprehension, satisfying the demand of unity in the Christian consciousness, and in the activity of the dialectic reason." (History of the Christian Church, Torrey's translation, I. 572 – 574.)

On the sentence last quoted, Dr. Huntington remarks: —

"Neander's historical judgment expressed in this passage, and sustained through his great work, will probably present itself as some offset in point of authority, to the assertion of those who say that the Trinity was unknown to the early Christian centuries."

Here let us have an understanding of terms. Those who say that the Trinity was unknown to the early Christian centuries, mean by "the Trinity" the doctrine, as it is expressed in the Assembly's Shorter Catechism, that " there are three persons in the Godhead, the Father, the Son, and the Holy Ghost, and these three are one God, the same in substance, equal in power and glory." This is now, I suppose, the prevalent form of the " ontological" doctrine of the Trinity. It is, as I understand it, the doctrine of Dr. Huntington, though he connects with it some other remarkable propositions. He maintains, for example, that the Son is "eternally begotten of the Father," and at the same time, that " his personality is *self-existent* and supreme;" that prayer to him is a "*richer* worship" than prayer to the Father; that when "the Saviour suffered, God suffered," and not merely "the second person of the divine Tri-unity," but that it was " as if *the Father* said, ... Lo! one mercy more, the last and mightiest. I can suffer for my children, I can come in the flesh, I can be one of them. In that incarnation I can ache and weep and sorrow for them and with them: all their stripes can be laid upon me. All their infirmities can cling to me. I can *die* as they die." (Christian Believing and Living, pp. 362, 524, 528, 390, 394.) On these views I have no desire to comment. I respect profoundly the earnest religious feeling with which they are connected in Dr. Huntington's mind; and I am willing that all readers should judge for themselves of their resemblance to the teachings of Christ and his Apostles. I cannot suppose that it will be pretended by any one that *these* propositions have been the common faith of the Christian Church in all ages and nations. I therefore confine my inquiry to the simple question, Was the doctrine of the Trinity, as above defined, generally received by Christians in the early centuries? And, in particular, Does *Neander* represent this to have been the case?

Neander, in the first volume of his Church History, pp. 574 – 610 of Torrey's translation, traces the *development* of the doctrine of the Trinity in the first three centuries. After alluding to "the form in which the Logos-idea was taught and transmitted in the tradition of the Church," "namely, as the idea of a spirit, first begotten of God and *subordinate to* him," he goes on to remark that "there was besides this, another view of the doctrine concerning the Trinity, which may be designated, after the customary language of this period, as that of the *Monarchians*." "They felt a common interest in preserving the unity of the consciousness of God, which made them unwilling to acknowledge any other divine being besides one God, the Father." Neander explains their opposition to the "hypostatical Logos-doctrine" by the fact that "the doctrine of the divine unity had been deeply impressed on their minds by the earliest catechetical instruction which they received, and that the Logos-idea did not originally belong to the primitive, simple confession of faith at baptism, as in fact it does not occur in the so-called Apostolic Creed."

How defective their doctrinal instruction must have been! He cites in a note the following passage of Tertullian, which I will translate, as it throws some light on the question about the prevalence of the doctrine of the Trinity in the early ages. Tertullian says: —

"All the simple, not to call them unwise and unlearned, *who always constitute the majority of believers,* since the rule of faith itself leads them from the many gods of the heathen world to the one true God, are startled at the doctrine of a Trinity...... We, they say, maintain the monarchy." (Adv. Praxeam, c. 3.)

Tertullian, who bears such unsuspicious testimony to the Unitarianism of the majority of Christians in his day, flourished A. D. 200. This testimony of Tertullian is confirmed by Origen, who flourished A. D. 230, in a striking passage to which Neander refers, and of which he gives the original (in part) in a note (p. 578). Origen says: —

"There are some who partake of the Logos that was in the beginning, the Logos that was with God, and was God; ..... but others, who know nothing but Jesus Christ and him crucified, thinking that the Logos made flesh is the whole of the Logos, are acquainted with Christ only according to the flesh. To this class belong *the great body of those who are considered believers.*" (In Joann. T. II. c. 3. Opp. IV. 53.)

Poor, benighted Christians! "knowing," like Paul, "nothing but Jesus Christ and him crucified"! who had not studied the philosophy of the Platonists, and had no relish for the lofty speculations of Origen and his school concerning the Logos before the incarnation, but (as Neander understands it) identified the Logos, that is, what was divine in Christ, with the Father!

After what has been stated, we need not be altogether surprised at the remark of Neander (p. 579), that "Monarchians of the third century appeal to the agreement of the older Roman bishops with their views." Though, as he observes, "modern inquirers have been led to infer from this circumstance, that the Monarchian tenet was in this Church originally the prevailing one, while the doctrine of the Logos was unknown to it," Neander takes a different view. He supposes that " they simply took advantage of *the more crude and undigested form* of the doctrine in the Roman Church to introduce their own." (p. 580.) I do not care to contend for anything more than he concedes.

It is impossible in a newspaper article to go into full details and explanations; but no one can read intelligently the account which Neander gives of the different classes of the Monarchians (pp. 576 – 585), without perceiving that they were very numerous. I know of no reason to doubt that Tertullian and Origen were correct in speaking of them as constituting the majority of believers, that is, of Gentile Christians. As to the Ebionites, or Jewish Christians, who early separated themselves from the former, it is well known that they universally rejected the doctrine of the deity of Christ.

I will now go on with a quotation from Neander. He says: —

" In the conflict with these two classes of the Monarchians, the Church doctrine of the Trinity unfolded itself, and in two different quarters, in the Western and in the Eastern Church. In the latter, the doctrine of *subordination* became firmly established in connection with the hypostatical view of the Logos [i. e. the view which regarded the Logos as a person, not an attribute of God]; since in the controversy with the Monarchians, who denied the distinction of hypostases, that distinction became still more prominently set forth. On the other hand, we see how the Western mind, starting from the doctrine of subordination received along with the distinction of hypostases, is ever striving to make prominent the unity of the divine essence in connection with this distinction. The designation of Christ as the Logos could have been known from the Gospel of John, without any use being made of it, however, for a speculative exposition of the doctrine concerning Christ. *This first took place*, when a species of intellectual culture which had been formed in the schools of philosophy, particularly in the Platonic school, ... came into contact with Christianity. The first author still extant, in whom this character may be discerned, is Justin Martyr. He availed himself, in his speculations (as Philo, whose ideas seem to have been known to him and to have influenced him, had already done), of the ambiguity of the Greek term Logos, which denotes both *reason* and *word*." (p. 585.)

Here Neander admits that the doctrine of *subordination*, that is, in plain English, the doctrine of the inferiority of the Son to the Father, characterized the Church doctrine of the Trinity, both in the East and the West. This is confirmed by his more detailed statements, and by all the passages he cites from the Fathers. Of this fact I will give a few illustrations.

In regard to Justin, who flourished A. D. 140 or 150, I will quote, for brevity, from the monograph of Semisch on his "Life, Writings, and Opinions," to which Neander refers (p. 609, note) as "remarkably full and thorough," premising that Semisch is a strong Trinitarian. He says: —

"The sense in which Justin believed that the Logos was subordinate to the Father, is twofold, — that of *complete dependence*, and of a *quantitative inequality of being*." (Semisch's *Justin Martyr*, II. 191, Ryland's translation.)

I wish I had space to cite a part of the overwhelming evidence of this fact, which Semisch produces from the writings of Justin. I cannot do this, but I will quote from him a sentence or two, on another important point. He says: —

"Justin considers the divine in Jesus as originally a pure property [*or* mere attribute], and subsequently a hypostasized power of Reason of God; accordingly he ascribes eternity to the Logos as a property, but not as a person. As long as the Logos rested in God, it was essentially identical with his substance, or rather stood in the relation of a part to the whole; by coming forth from the divine essence, it first attained a personal self-subsistence. Justin entertained the opinion which is so briefly expressed by Tertullian: *fuit tempus cum filius non fuit* [i. e. "there was a time when the Son was not"], and supposed that the creation of the world was the epoch when the Logos came forth from God." (*Ibid.*, p. 181.)

"We find in the other apologetic writers," namely, Tatian, Athenagoras, and Theophilus of Antioch, as Neander remarks, "the same fundamental view" as in Justin; and he notices in the case of Athenagoras, that

"He is led to express himself on the unity of the divine essence, in a way which strikes a middle course between the Monarchian theory and the doctrine of the Church in its later and more matured form. It is easy to see how the above-named Monarchians might avail themselves of the authority of such passages, to maintain the higher antiquity of their own form of doctrine." (p. 586.)

"Thus unfolded," Neander goes on to observe, "this doctrine passed over into the Alexandrian school." — "The Alexandrian system, which sprang out of the germ furnished by Clement, was first carried out and moulded into its perfect shape by Origen; — and the influence of his exposition of the doctrine continued long to be felt in the Eastern Church." (pp. 586, 587.) In opposition to the notion which had been prevalent "of an emanation of the Logos to self-subsistent existence before the creation of the world," Origen maintained his eternal, or rather timeless generation. This was demanded by his philosophy. "He," as Neander remarks, "who fixed no beginning to the *creation*, but supposed it to be eternal, would far less fix any beginning here." (p. 588.)

But Origen never dreamed of making the Logos *equal* with the Father. As Neander observes: —

"It appeared to him something like a profanation of the first and supreme essence, to suppose an equality of essence or a unity between Him and any other being whatever, not excepting even the Son of God. As the Son of God and the Holy Spirit are incomparably exalted above all other existences, even in the highest ranks of the spiritual world, *so high and yet higher is the Father exalted even above them.*" (In Joann. T. XIII. c. 25. Opp. IV. 235.)

"From this doctrine he drew the practical inference, that we are bound to pray to the Father alone, and not to the Son." (p. 590.)

I pass over the account which Neander gives (pp. 591–605) of the opinions of Beryllus, Sabellius, and Paul of Samosata, all opposed to the doctrine of the Trinity, yet having many adherents. We will glance at the development of the doctrine in the Western Church, as represented by Tertullian. Neander remarks (p. 605):—

"He could quite clearly conceive, by the aid of his material notions of emanation, how the Godhead might cause to proceed from its own essence a being possessed of the same substance, only *in an inferior degree*, and standing in the same relation to the former as a ray of light to the sun. He asserted, therefore, the doctrine of *one* divine Essence, shared in a certain *gradation* by three persons, most intimately connected.

"The Son, so far as it concerns the divine essence, is not numerically distinct from the Father; the same essence of God being also in the Son; but he differs in degree, being a *smaller portion* of the common mass of the divine essence. Thus the prevailing view in the Western Church came to be this: one divine essence in the Father and Son; but, at the same time, a *subordination* in the relation of the Son to the Father." (p. 605.)

Neander proceeds to mention the fact, that the Council of Antioch, A. D. 269, *condemned* the famous expression *homoousios*, "consubstantial," which was made the test of orthodoxy at the Council of Nice, A. D. 325. He then gives an account of a friendly discussion, remarkably free from personalities, between Dionysius, Bishop of Alexandria, and Dionysius, Bishop of Rome. The former, as Neander remarks,

"Made use of several expressions which Arianism could afterwards fall back upon. He made it a prominent point that the Son of God had his existence by the will of the Father; he styled the Son, in relation to the latter, a ποίημα, [*i. e.* "work," "creature,"] and employed many singular comparisons with a view to mark his subordinate relation to the Father." (p. 606.)

The views of Dionysius of Rome were somewhat nearer to the orthodoxy of later times. There is nothing, however, in what remains to us of his writings, which approaches the doctrine of a Trinity of coequal persons. On the contrary, as Neander admits (p. 607, note), he clearly recognizes the subordination of the Son, and the supremacy of the Father, as "the Head of the divine Triad, the Almighty God of the Universe."

Neander goes on to remark: —

"In the doctrine concerning the *Holy Spirit*, the want of correspondence between what was contained in the Christian consciousness and its notional expression clearly manifested itself. In the first youthful age of the Church, when the power of the Holy Spirit made itself to be so mightily felt in the life, as a new creative, transforming principle, it was still very far from being the case that the consciousness of this Spirit, as one identical with the essence of God, had been thoroughly apprehended and presented in conceptions of the understanding.

"If we except the Monarchians and *Lactantius*, men were agreed in conceiving of the Holy Spirit as a personal being. . . . . But the logical consistency of their system of subordination in the Logos-doctrine, compelled the Church Fathers to conceive of the Holy Spirit as *subordinate to the Father and the Son; the first of the beings produced by the Father through the Son;* — and we shall perceive the after influence of this tendency of thought in the Eastern Church till late into the fourth century." "In Justin Martyr, particularly, we may observe a wavering between the idea of the Holy Ghost as one of the members of the Triad, and a spirit standing in some relationship with the angels." "In Origen we observe two elements coming together, the sound *Christian* view, producing itself out of the immediate contents of the Christian consciousness, and the speculative view, standing in no sort of relation to it. On the one hand, he considers the Holy Spirit as the substance of all the gracious gifts proceeding from God, communicated through Christ, the source of sanctification to believers; and then he describes him, notwithstanding, as only the first-begotten of the Father through the Son, to whom not only being, but also wisdom and holiness, is first communicated by the Son, dependent on him in all these relations.

"It is besides worthy of notice, that, in the dispute with the Monarchians, the doctrine concerning the Holy Spirit was not touched upon at all,— a proof how little men had busied themselves, as yet, with the more accurate determination of this doctrine." (pp. 608 – 610.)

Such is an outline of the account which Neander gives of the development of the doctrine of the Trinity in the first three centuries. He mentions not *a single writer*, however eccentric, within that period, to whom he ascribes the doctrine of "a Trinity of coequal persons." How remote from that doctrine are the opinions which he does describe as prevalent, every reader must have perceived. What, then, are we to think of the assertion of Dr. Huntington, quoted near the beginning of this article? Did he understand the passage of Neander to which he refers?

We have no space left for a sketch of the development of the doctrine of the Trinity in the *fourth* century, the age of the Arian controversy. In the early part of this century Christianity became the religion of the state; a new and most potent cause, in addition to others which were before in operation, of its rapid debasement and corruption. It was towards the end of this century, that, after most violent struggles, during which

> "Long time in even scale
> The battle hung,"

something like the present doctrine of the Trinity was first embodied in a creed, and established as orthodox by the irresistible authority of the Emperor Theodosius. E. A.

VII.

THE DOCTRINE OF THE TRINITY IN THE FOURTH CENTURY.

MR. EDITOR:—In the Register of last week I stated and illustrated the fact, that the doctrine of "a Trinity of coequal persons," which Dr. Huntington calls "the sublime working-scheme of Revelation and Redemption" (Christian Believing, &c., p. 364), was unknown to the Christian Church of the first three centuries. The simplicity of the primitive faith had certainly become corrupted; but *that* conception, so far as appears, had never entered the mind of even a single individual who flourished in this period. For the proof of this fact I confined myself almost wholly to the Church History of the Trinitarian Neander, to which Dr. Huntington had appealed. But it may be well to remark that other Trinitarian scholars of the highest eminence, as Petavius, Huet, Beausobre, and Cudworth, admit that the inferiority of the Son to the Father was the common doctrine of the Christian writers who preceded the Council of Nice.

Taking Neander again as a guide, I now propose to notice, as briefly as possible, the development of the doctrine of the Trinity in the *fourth* century. I shall enter but little into detail. The subject will be found treated in Neander's Church History, Vol. II. pp. 360 – 420 of Torrey's translation.

The famous Council of Nice was convoked by the Emperor Constantine, A. D. 325, for the purpose, in part, of settling the dispute between Alexander, Bishop of Alexandria, and his presbyter, Arius. The point at issue was this, — Whether the Son was begotten from eternity, of the same substance with the Father, or whether he was created out of nothing. The majority of the Council, as Neander states (pp. 372, 373), occupied a middle ground between the parties, entertaining views similar to those of Eusebius of Cæsarea, being ready to declare the Son to be of *like* substance with the Father, exalted above all other beings, but objecting to the term *homoousios*, "consubstantial," which had been rejected by an earlier Council. The Emperor, however, under the influence of Hosius and his associates, decided in favor of this term, and his will was law. His decision was the more readily submitted to, as the word in question admitted of different interpretations. But as Neander justly remarks: —

"The manner in which the controversies had been decided by the Council of Nice could only contain the seeds for new disputes; for there was here no cordial union springing freely, by a natural course of development, out of inward conviction: but *a forced and artificial union of men*, still widely separated by their different modes of thinking, *on a creed which had been imposed on them*, and which was differently expounded according to the different doctrinal interests of the several parties. Thus it happened, that while for the present no party ventured as yet to come out decidedly against the Homoousion [*sameness* of substance], still those who had received it, explaining it to mean Homoiousion [*likeness* of substance], accused the others, who interpreted it and held it fast in its proper and original signification, of Sabellianism; while the latter accused the former of Tritheism." "Yet the major part of the Eastern Church would naturally strive to rid themselves of the imposed articles of the Nicene Creed." (p. 378.)

I pass over the melancholy history of the contests between the Arians and their opponents for fifty years after the Council of Nice. In the year 328 Arius was recalled from banishment, and restored to favor with the Emperor. Athanasius was forced to spend twenty of the forty-six years of his bishopric in exile or concealment. Numerous and influential councils favored Arian or Eusebian opinions; and during far the greater part of the period to which I refer, these opinions were predominant in the Eastern Church, while the Nicene doctrine, on the other hand, had the ascendency in the West. But the most important fact to be attended to is, that even the Nicene Creed is not Trinitarian. As Professor Stuart remarks:—

"It presents the Father as the *Monas*, the Divinity or proper Godhead in and of himself exclusively; it represents him as the *Fons et Principium* of the Son, and therefore gives him superior power and glory. It does not even assert the claims of the Blessed Spirit to Godhead: and therefore leaves room to doubt whether it means to recognize a *Trinity* or only a *Duality*." (*Biblical Repository* for April, 1835, Vol. V. p. 317.)

This leads me to quote, in further illustration of the gradual development of the doctrine of the Trinity, the following remarks of Neander:—

"It must excite surprise that the doctrine of the Holy Spirit is only adverted to in very general terms in the Nicene Creed. Why was the Homoousian doctrine not applied to it? It has been alleged that at that time there was no controversy respecting it. *But this ground is not correct;* for it is evident from the express statement of Athanasius, that Arius applied the doctrine of subordination to the Holy Spirit; he placed the same distance between the Son and the Spirit as between the Father and the Son. According to him, the Holy Spirit was only the first of created beings, brought into existence by the Son as the organ of the Father. Or should we be justified in saying that attention had not been sufficiently directed to this point? that it was not held to be of sufficient importance? The true reason rather consists in this, that the Oriental Church *was at that time much less fitted to admit the Homoousia* [consubstantiality] *of the Holy Spirit as part of its doctrine,* and if it had been urged, *its opposition against the Homoousion would have been still greater.* ..... But even as late as A. D. 380, great indistinctness prevailed among different parties respecting this dogma, so that even GREGORY NAZIANZEN could say, 'Some of our theologians regard the Spirit simply as a mode of divine operation, others as a creature of God, others as God himself; others, again, say that they know not which of these opinions to accept, from their reverence for Holy Writ, which says nothing upon it.' HILARY of Poictiers, a Nicene theologian, acknowledges that the Holy Ghost exists, and that faith in him is necessarily connected with confessing the Father and the Son, and to know this is sufficient. If any one ask what the Holy Spirit is, and is not satisfied that he is through Him and from Him through whom are all things; that he is the Spirit of God, and his gift to believers, even Apostles and Prophets will not satisfy such a person, for they only assert this of him, that he *is*. He does not venture to attribute to him the name God, because the Scripture does not so call him expressly, yet [as] it says, that the Holy Spirit searcheth the deep things of God, it follows that he partakes of the divine essence. Though BASIL of Cæsarea [fl. A. D. 370] wished to teach the divinity of the Holy Spirit in his church, he *only ventured to introduce it gradually*. The subject was brought more distinctly under discussion, when many of the Homoiousians showed themselves ready to adopt the Nicene doctrine, but could not make up their minds to extend the Homoousion to the Holy Spirit. In order to remove their objections, Athanasius, who from the first had been consequential on this dogma, composed his letter to Serapion, Bishop of Thmuis." (Neander's *Hist. of Christian Dogmas*, I. 303 – 305; compare his *Church History*, II. 418 – 423.)

The merits of Athanasius in discovering and establishing the Trinitarian doctrine respecting the Holy Spirit are stated in a striking manner by Gregory Nazianzen. I will quote a short, but important passage from his Eulogy on this great champion of Orthodoxy. He says of Athanasius: —

"When all others who held our doctrine were divided into three classes, the faith of many being unsound respecting the Son, that of still more concerning the Holy Spirit (on which subject to be least impious was thought to be piety), and a small number being sound in both respects; *he first and alone, or with a very few,* had the courage to profess in writing, clearly and explicitly, the true doctrine of the one Godhead and nature of the three persons. Thus that truth, a knowledge of which, as far as regards the Son, had been vouchsafed to most of the Fathers before, he was fully *inspired* to maintain in respect to the Holy Spirit." (*Orat.* XXI. c. 34. Opp. I. 408, as translated by Mr. Norton, *Statement of Reasons*, 3d ed., pp. 43, 44.)

The statements which have thus far been made respecting the history of the doctrine of the Holy Spirit, are all, as the reader will observe, *concessions of Trinitarian writers.* It must not be supposed that they present a full view of the evidence that the proper Trinitarian doctrine on this subject was unknown in the early ages of the Christian Church. They are, however, amply sufficient for my purpose. But I wish to just notice a single other point, suggested by the manner in which Dr. Huntington closes his sermon on the Trinity, in his "Christian Believing," &c., p. 412, and his sermon on the Divinity of Christ, in his "Sermons for the People," p. 270. An ascription of glory or praise to two or three beings in connection does not prove that the person who makes it regards them as equal, much less that he believes in their deity. But considering the facts admitted by Neander and Gregory Nazianzen, it may be suspected that there is some foundation for the explicit statement of the ecclesiastical historian Philostorgius, (fl. A. D. 425,) though an Arian, that

"Flavian of Antioch [who flourished A. D. 381] was the first who, having collected together a large band of monks, shouted aloud the doxology, 'Glory be to the Father, *and* to the Son, *and* to the Holy Spirit.' For among those who preceded him, some had been accustomed to say, 'Glory be to the Father, *through* the Son, *in* the Holy Spirit,' and this latter form of doxology was the one generally received; while others again used a different form, saying, 'Glory be to the Father, *in* the Son, and *in* the Holy Spirit.'" (*Hist. Eccles.* III. 13.)

An Illyrian council held in the year 375, as Neander remarks (Church History, II. 420, note 3), "was the first to extend the *homoousion* [consubstantiality] to the doctrine concerning the Holy Spirit." The Council of Constantinople, the second general council, summoned by the Emperor Theodosius, A. D. 381, supplied the deficiency in the Nicene Creed, which simply says, "I believe in the Holy Spirit," by adding the words, "the Lord, the Giver of Life, who proceeds from the Father, who together with the Father and the Son is worshipped and glorified, who spoke by the prophets." It may be worth while to note, though unimportant for the present purpose, that the expressions "the Lord, the giver of life," are founded on a misunderstanding of 2 Cor. iii. 17 and John vi. 63.

Something *like* the present orthodox doctrine of the Trinity was now established, and its reception was enforced with unrelenting severity by the imperial power. I say something *like* it; for the Nicene creed, as enlarged at Constantinople, does not expressly teach the *equality* of the three persons, or their *numerical unity*. This development of the doctrine was, however, soon attained. As Gieseler remarks: —

" The unity and equality of the persons, which necessarily resulted from holding sameness of essence, was not fully acknowledged at once even by the Nicenians, but continued [came] to be more clearly perceived, until at last it was expressed by *Augustine* for the first time with decided logical consequence." (*Church History*, 4th ed., § 83 ; Vol. I. p. 313 of Davidson's translation, Amer. edition.)

The doctrine of the Trinity, essentially in the form in which it was established in the Latin Church by the powerful influence of Augustine, is embodied in that remarkable document which has been known by the name of "the Athanasian creed," or the "Symbolum *Quicunque*," from the word with which it commences. When or by whom this creed was composed, nobody knows ; but an earlier date cannot possibly be assigned to it than the latter part of the fifth century. It was undoubtedly originally written in Latin, not in Greek. Neander conjectures that Vigilius of Tapsus, in North Africa, a noted literary forger, was the author. It begins by informing the reader, that unless he receives the doctrine therein contained, and keeps it whole and undefiled, " without doubt he shall perish everlastingly."

The doctrine of the procession of the Holy Spirit "from the Father *and the Son*," was first publicly sanctioned by the authority of the Council of Toledo, A. D. 589. It has never been received by the Greek Church.

The present orthodox doctrine of the Trinity — that of the Westminster Confession and of the Protestant creeds generally — has undoubtedly been prevalent in the Roman Church since the time of Augustine. But, as Cudworth remarks, it "seemeth not to have been owned by any public authority in the Christian Church save that of the Lateran Council only." (Intellectual System, I. 793, Andover ed.) He refers to the fourth general Lateran council, held in 1215, under Pope Innocent III. This council, at the same time, established likewise the doctrine of Transubstantiation.

If the account which Neander gives of the doctrine of the Trinity in the first four centuries is correct, the careful reader will perceive that the main argument of Dr. Huntington's sermon falls at once to the ground. Much more might be said to show the falsity of the assumptions on which that argument is founded; but nothing more can be needed.

E. A.

VIII.

FURTHER ILLUSTRATIONS OF NEANDER'S VIEWS, AND OF DR. HUNTINGTON'S QUOTATIONS, WITH A PRACTICAL IMPROVEMENT OF THE SUBJECT.

MR. EDITOR: — With regard to Neander, it will be remembered that the points on which I have insisted are these: — 1. That he makes a broad distinction between what he calls " the *practical* doctrine of the Trinity," and " the *speculative* or *ontological*," regarding the former alone as " the basis of the true unity of the Church," and, in fact, universally received by Christians. 2. That his " practical doctrine of the Trinity," as he explains it, is purely *Unitarian*.

Dr. Huntington, in his letter published in the Register of Feb. 4, cites Neander as follows: —

"He not only affirms that 'the essence of all Christianity is contained in it,' but that the doctrine of the Trinity is 'the *perfect development of the doctrine about Christ;*' and 'that it is *rooted in the centre-point of Christianity.*'" (The Italics are his.)

Dr. Huntington did not inform his readers where the passages thus quoted from Neander were to be found. They are taken from the *first* edition of the first volume of his Church History, as translated by Rose, which was published in London in 1841, and reprinted in Philadelphia in 1843. In the greatly enlarged *second* edition, translated by Torrey, the corresponding paragraph (I. 571 – 573) is entirely rewritten. The larger part of *this* was given in the Register of Jan. 21. I do not object to Dr. Huntington's quoting from the first edition rather than the second, as Neander's views on the matter in question are essentially the same in both; but it would have been a convenience to some of his readers to have been notified of the fact, that part of his citations from this volume of Neander's History were from one edition, and part from another.

In the article published in the Register of Feb. 11, I simply remarked that these quotations by Dr. Huntington did not in the slightest degree invalidate any statement I had made. I now propose to confirm this assertion by quoting the whole paragraph from which they were taken. I do so for two reasons; first, because the sentiments therein expressed by Neander are so excellent in themselves, and so important in their practical bearings; and secondly, because it may be satisfactory to your readers to see the somewhat fragmentary quotations of Dr. Huntington *in situ*, as the geologists say. I will only add, that I believe Rose's translation to be substantially correct, though the meaning might sometimes be more clearly brought out by a change of expression. I have accordingly substituted "contents" for "import," as the rendering of *Inhalt*, and have suggested a few other slight changes in brackets.

The following is the paragraph in question: —

"The peculiar nature [essence] of Christianity reveals itself in the recognition and worship of God, not merely as the Creator, but also as the Redeemer and Sanctifier of human nature, in the belief that God, who has created human nature pure, has redeemed it when it became estranged from him by sin, and continues [will continue] to sanctify it, until it shall have attained in an eternal life to an untroubled and beatified communion with him in perfect holiness. Without this faith and knowledge, there is no lively worship of God, no worship of God in spirit and in truth, because a lively worship of God cannot exist without communion with him, and because this communion cannot be shared by man, as long as he is estranged from God by sin; as long as that which separates him from God is not removed; and because the worship of God in spirit and in truth can only proceed from a soul which has been sanctified so as to become a temple of God. This doctrine of *God*, the *Creator*, the *Redeemer*, and the *Sanctifier* of human nature, is the essential contents of the doctrine of the *Trinity*, and therefore, since [since therefore] in this latter doctrine the essence of all Christianity is contained, it could not but happen, that as this doctrine proceeded out of [when this doctrine came forth from] the depths of Christian consciousness, it should be considered as the chief doctrine of Christianity, and that even in the earliest Church the essential contents of the faith should be annexed to the doctrine of the Father, the Son, and the Holy Ghost. This doctrine again is nothing else than the doctrine of God, who has revealed and imparted himself to sinful man in Christ; everything here reverts to the doctrine of God's being in Christ, for the working of God in human nature redeemed by him, presupposes the inward relation, into which God has entered with human nature through Christ, and all is here only the continuation and consequence of that relation; and therefore this doctrine [i.e. of God the Creator, Redeemer, and Sanctifier of human nature], is nothing else but the perfect development of the doctrine about Christ, which the Apostle Paul, 1 Corinthians iii. calls the foundation of all Christianity, the development of that which Christ himself designates as the essential contents of his doctrine: 'This is eternal life, that they should know thee, that thou alone art the true God, and Jesus Christ whom thou hast sent.' But the *speculative* doctrine of the Trinity is carefully to be distinguished from *this* its essential Christian contents, and men might agree in the latter, and yet differ from each other in their conceptions of the former. The former only set itself up as *a human attempt* to bring into just harmony with the unity of the Divine Being, the existence of God in Christ, and through Christ in the faithful, as it is represented in Holy Scripture, and out of that Scripture formed an image of itself in the inward life and the inward perceptions of the faithful. But it was an evil that, in this attempt, men did not rightly divide the speculative and dialectic element from that essential and practical foundation; the consequence of which was, that men transplanted that doctrine from *its proper practical ground in which* it is rooted in the centre point of Christianity, into a speculative region foreign to it, which might give an opportunity of mingling with it much extraneous matter, and again might lead to setting Christianity, contrary to its peculiar character, on a speculative instead of a practical foundation; and the consequence of this again was, that men, overprizing the importance of speculative differences, *tore asun-*

der the bond of Christian communion, where there was yet an agreement in what is practical and essential; and on the other hand, that men stinted the *free development* of the Christian doctrine, by the attempt to *attain a uniformity of speculative* conceptions." (Neander's *Hist. of the Christian Church*, (1st ed.) Rose's translation, p. 368 of the Amer. ed., corresponding to pp. 986 – 988 of the original.)

I need not remark how completely this passage agrees with all I have stated as to the views of Neander. Its dangerous tendency was perceived by the translator, who thought it necessary to give a warning to the reader in the following curious note: —

" We must also be careful that in endeavoring to reconcile contending views we do not depart from the great truth which is contained in the Athanasian Creed, that each person is acknowledged 'by himself to be both God and Lord, and yet that no one should for a moment believe that there be three Gods or three Lords.' We must take care that we do not explain the Divinity of the Son as the mere indwelling of the Father in Jesus Christ; or believe that the Son is the mere manifestation of the Father; or we shall fall into Sabellianism or Patripassianism at once. The evil which Neander wishes to obviate, seems to be the attempt to *explain* this great truth *speculatively*, and creating differences in consequence of such attempts. [?] However wrong such attempts may be, in opposing them we must still be careful to maintain that great Catholic truth, the Trinity in Unity, and the Unity in Trinity, which is founded on the Scriptures, and must be received by faith, though our finite faculties are unable to explain its mysteries. — H. J. R."

In the Register of Feb. 4, Dr. Huntington explains the misquotation of Neander, in his sermon on the Trinity, by saying that

"The quotation was transferred from an article by a theological writer, whose accuracy I had no reason to question, and whose honesty is above suspicion, where many of the readers of the 'Register' must have seen it."

In justice to the eminent writer of the article referred to, it should be stated that he is responsible for only *one* of the mistakes made by Dr. Huntington in quoting this unlucky passage. His language was this:—

"Neander calls it [the article of the Trinity] 'the fundamental article of the Christian faith; and we recognize therein,' he says, 'the essential contents of Christianity summed up in brief.'"

Dr. Huntington (p. 378), not observing that the words "and we recognize *therein*" were essential to a true representation of Neander's meaning, omitted them, making Neander assert that the article of the Trinity "*is* the essential contents of Christianity summed up in brief." Under the circumstances, misled as he was as to Neander's view by his friend's misquotation of the first clause, this inadvertence was very natural and excusable. But I did marvel that he did not perceive the error when it was distinctly pointed out.

But let us drop these comparatively trivial matters, and turn our attention to the practical bearing of Neander's view of the *importance* of the doctrine of the Trinity, as contrasted with that of Dr. Huntington.

If, as Dr. Huntington maintains (pp. 355, 356), the doctrine of "a Trinity of coequal persons," each of whom is to be worshipped as God, is "the fundamental article of Christian belief," announced by our Saviour as "the one essential characteristic truth of his religion," if this constitutes the creed which he gave his Church at the close of his earthly ministry, it necessarily follows that no one who rejects this doctrine is entitled to the name of Christian. Among those who have rejected it, there may be, indeed, some who are " honorable in character " (p. 361), even "devout," being " exceptional cases," "indebted after all to hereditary influences which they do not acknowledge" (p. 402); but they are out of the pale of the Christian Church. They must be excluded from Christian fellowship. Such men as Newton and Locke, Clarke and Lardner, Priestley and Price, Cappe and Carpenter, Buckminster and Channing, Worcester and Tuckerman, Freeman and Greenwood, the Wares and the Peabodys, Norton and Nichols, and such women as Mrs. Ware and Florence Nightingale, can at best be regarded only as religious Deists.

I do not say that Dr. Huntington expressly affirms this. The inference may be logically inevitable from his premises; but it would be very unsafe to assume, on that account, that he makes it. It is an inference, however, that *has* been made and acted upon by the great body of Trinitarians.

But if, on the other hand, as Neander maintains, " the doctrine of the Trinity does *not* belong to the fundamental articles of the Christian faith," being expressly taught in no passage of the New Testament; if the only doctrine which the Head of the Church and his Apostles pronounced fundamental is cordially received by Unitarians; if, in fact, their faith embraces the *essence* of the doctrine of the Trinity itself, all that gives it any practical value, namely, " the recognition of God not merely as the Creator, but also as the Redeemer and Sanctifier of humanity;" then Unitarians who acknowledge Jesus as their Lord are not infidels. It is the plain duty of all Christians to welcome them heartily to their fellowship as brethren. To refuse to do this, is, as Neander expresses it, " to tear asunder the bond of Christian communion, where there is yet an agreement in what is practical and essential."

And it is more than this. If Jesus Christ and his Apostles have required for admission to the Church no other confession of faith but this, that Jesus is the Anointed of God; if, in other words, to be a Christian believer is simply to acknowledge the divine authority of Christ as our Lord and Master in religion, what shall we say to our Protestant Popes, the imposers of metaphysical creeds? You set aside as insufficient the foundation on which Christ and his Apostles built the Church. For the only doctrine which they declared fundamental, you substitute that of a Trinity of co-equal persons in the Godhead, a human speculation of which we find no trace in Christian history for more than three hundred years after Christ. Who gave you the keys of the kingdom of Heaven? Show us your credentials. Is it possible that you, mere fallible men, have presumed to do this, without an express commission from God?

E. A.

THE PRIMITIVE CHRISTIAN CREED.

By ORVILLE DEWEY, D. D.

"Go ye, therefore, and teach all nations, baptizing them in the name of the Father, and of the Son, and of the Holy Ghost." — Matthew xxviii. 19.

These words set forth the primitive creed of Christianity. As they have been fully discussed of late, both by the pulpit and the press, I hasten to say that I do not propose to enter into any speculative controversy about them. I am quite content with the discussion which has lately been given them on our part;* and my design is simply to follow that discussion, with some thoughts upon their positive and vital meaning and significance.

All formulas are liable, through constant repetition, to lose the sense which they originally conveyed. Unending scholastic controversy has increased the tendency in this case. And as we reject the common, Church construction, we are the more liable not sufficiently to consider the stupendous burden of meaning which is borne by the words, "Father, Son, and Holy Ghost." Just as the word "Trinity" has so little in it of the divine idea and essence, that it can be freely applied to a building, — to a college or church. We could not say — pointing to a building — this is the God College

---

* I mean, in the foregoing volume.

or the God Church. But we say, Trinity Church or Trinity College, because the word is a mere abstraction.

But the form of words in our text, is, in its true meaning, the farthest possible from being an abstraction. I know not any words in language, of such depth and vitality as these. And I would fain do something to rescue them from that hard, abstract, and conventional sense which controversy and constant usage have given them; and would awaken, if I could, some new, fresh, and living apprehension of their power and beauty.

The great, original, and peculiar creed of Christianity, I say, is the doctrine of the Father, of the Son, and of the Holy Ghost. For the *unity* and *spirituality* of God are not the peculiar teachings of Christianity. *They* had been taught in the Hebrew system. But that God, the Infinite Being, is our Father; that Jesus Christ is the highest son of God, the highest manifestation and image of the Divine; and that there is a spirit and power of God, manifested in the world and in human souls; — these are the strong reliances, the supporting pillars, of our Christian faith.

The Teacher had instructed his disciples; he had instructed them on purpose to make them missionaries to the nations; and now, about to part from them, he gives them this solemn charge: "Go and teach all nations," — the word translated "teach" means, as you know, to disciple, or make disciples of, — "baptizing them in, or into, the name" — i. e. into the acknowledgment — "of the Father, and of the Son, and of the Holy Ghost." Baptism — laving with water — had long been used as an expressive symbol of inward purification, not only among the Hebrews, but among many other nations. And there is reason to believe, though it has been made a subject of learned question, that for some centuries before the time of Christ, baptism had been among the Jews the specific proselyte's rite, — the rite, i. e. applied to converts from heathenism, as an emblem of the inward purification required of them. It is observable that our Saviour adopts the words without explanation, as if their use was familiar and their meaning well understood. As men had been baptized, and by that formal act visibly received into the bosom of Judaism, so were they now to be baptized, i. e. openly brought into the bosom of Christianity; and the sum of Christianity is here set forth as the doctrine and power in the soul, of the Father, Son, and Spirit.

This language, I may observe in passing, carries with it demonstrative proof that the Gospel, in the mind of Jesus, was more than a system of natural religion; that he himself was more than a mere human teacher, like Socrates or Confucius, or even like David or Isaiah. Not to say that his language everywhere implied such a consciousness of union with God as no other being on earth ever felt, what blasphemy must it not have been, *without* that consciousness, to have placed himself in such a relation, to have put his name into that awful formula! Imagine any other person — imagine John to have said, "In the name of the Father, and of *John*, and of the Holy Ghost"! If any one, to escape the conclusion, shall deny that Jesus ever used those words, — if he can believe that such a signal and final charge was either fabricated or falsified or misreported by the Evangelist, — then certainly *nothing* in the record can be relied upon as having been spoken by Christ; there is not a single shred of the historic, matter-of-fact New Testament left to hang to; and the whole grand and stable Christianity has no other basis than the vague and idle hearsay of mythic dreamers.

Let us now proceed to consider the separate articles of the great Christian Creed.

First, the doctrine of the Father: the doctrine that teaches us to address the Supreme Being, not with the title of Creator only, nor of Upholder, nor of Ruler, nor of Benefactor only, but by that most endearing of all names, a name indicative of a personal care and interest for his creatures,—the name of Father.

Let us trace for a moment the history of men's ideas of God, in order to see what place and value attach to our Christian idea. In the range of human opinion, there are two extremes, equally remote from this idea; they are known in philosophy under the names of *feticism* and *pantheism*. The first of these, marking the very beginnings of human thought, in some sort identified God with the mere visible fact and force of nature; the mountain, the ocean, the storm, the thunder, or the rudest and hugest idol, the most literal representation of material force, was, as it were, God to the rude children of the elder world. The other extreme, pantheism, was a later development of thought, and regarded God, not as a person at all, still less as an idol, but as the impersonal and unconscious essence of all nature and life. The extremes, you perceive, approach each other; feticism and pantheism alike approach to the worship of nature; but in passing from one to the other, there is an immense circle of thought, in which lie many and various forms of human faith. Beginning, that is to say, with the earliest and rudest form of thought, and coming down, we meet with polytheism, idolatry, anthropomorphism, the unity and spirituality of the divine nature, and, in later days, philosophic theism, falling and fading away into pantheism, i. e. into the notion of a diffused immensity of the Supreme Existence, which leaves no proper sense of its presence or inspection, or concern with human affairs.

Among these systems takes its pre-eminent place, the idea of a Father in heaven; of a God who is love; of an infinite and all-sustaining goodness, without whom not a sparrow falls to the ground, whose care extends to the humblest things on earth,— how much more to creatures of a rational and spiritual nature; and this great and sacred, this all-attractive and winning idea of the Supreme Nature, we receive and cherish as the first article of our Christian creed. Let us consider it.

In looking at the condition of the human race, I do not know that anything is more mysterious to me, than *that ignorance of God* which has prevailed over all the early ages, and, indeed, still prevails. That a being of infinite perfection and goodness should have suffered his creatures for ages to bow down to stocks and stones, to worship for himself the monsters of their own imagination; that he should suffer *now*, even in Christian lands, so many to be the slaves of superstition,— this is the mystery; and it is far more trying to my faith than it is to believe that he has interposed from time to time, to roll off this dark cloud of ignorance and this heavy burden of fear and misery from the world. What could more pain a noble-minded man, a good and kind parent, than to see himself so misapprehended by his children,—

to see them cowering around him with fear and dread, when all his heart was love and tenderness? It is a mystery, I say; and it is more trying to my faith than miracles. But this is what I have thought upon it: If the Infinite Parent saw that his earthly children *must* work up their way to light from an infancy of the race; that it was best for *them;* that it was the *only* way for them, as improvable, moral beings; that *such* fear was a better and juster sentiment than no fear at all; that human society, that the human race, could not subsist any way without it; and that *for* men and *to* men in their early ignorance, this exaggerated and superstitious fear was right, as being the best they could render; nay, more, that, as for worshipping a being of their own imagination or idea, they *must* worship such an one; that their worship *could* not advance beyond their culture; that *our own,* in fact, is but one stage of necessary imperfection; — then, I think, we may understand something of this great mystery.

But the ages slowly rolled on, constantly but slowly improving, till the old Hebrew prophets, standing in the centre of the then most cultivated world, — Egypt, Phœnicia, and Assyria lying around them, and almost within the reach of their voice, — proclaimed the unity and spirituality of God. And afterwards, it may incidentally be observed, Mahomet, on the same central theatre, took up the same great doctrine of the unity of God; and, though with violence and blood, he propagated it among nations that had not yet received it.

But the unity of God may consist with stupendous errors; the one God may, to the human mind, be as dreadful as many; and in the fulness of time came, by

Jesus Christ, the revelation of God as our Father in heaven. It is true, the ascription of that name had been heard before in the world. Among the Greeks and Romans the Supreme Being had been denominated "the Father Omnipotent;" "the Father of gods and men." And in the Hebrew Scriptures, we meet with those most tender and touching words, "Like as a father pitieth his children, so the Lord pitieth them that fear him; for he knoweth our frame, he remembereth that we are dust." Still in contradistinction to the Greek and Roman tone, and in a fuller unfolding of the Hebrew sense, Jesus taught that God is our Father. Still his teaching vindicated that which John averred, when he said, "No man hath seen God at any time; the only begotten Son, who is in the bosom of the Father, he hath declared him." No mortal teacher ever uttered the word "Father," when speaking of God, so frequently and so emphatically, or in such manner, as he did; from no human lips did it ever fall in such gracious and winning accents. "I thank thee, O *Father*, Lord of heaven and earth; even so, *Father*, for so it seemed good in thy sight; for I am in the *Father*, and the *Father* in me; I will pray the *Father* for you; O righteous *Father*, the world hath not known thee, but I have known thee, and these have known that thou hast sent me; O my *Father*, if it be possible, let this cup pass from me; I seek not mine own, but the will of my *Father*; I go to the *Father*, for my *Father* is greater than I." It is manifest that a new idea of God came into the world through this teaching. The sense of an infinite benignity reigning over us, the sense of an infinite love and pity encompassing us, came to the heart of the world as it never came before.

Of the value of this revelation, such is my view that it seems to me fitly to occupy the first place in the Christian creed; and that it is impossible to speak of it in any exaggerated terms. If the awful power that is above and around us is — Almighty indeed — but is Almighty LOVE; if an infinite goodness beams from every distant star and glows in the sunshine that falls upon my daily path; if an all-transcending loveliness is reflected in this fair creation around us; if it is indeed a boundless *love* of good and of beauty, that breathes in air, and blossoms in the flower, and waves in the trees, and hovers, like the dove of peace, over the trembling waters; if the "sweet heavens" have touched our hearts with tenderness and pity; if God, the Infinite God, is our Father, the parent-being who looks upon our being with ineffable kindness, having made it for the love and likeness of himself; — then what unutterable glory and beauty are here! Then, how does the sense of this love create, as the Scripture saith, a new heavens and a new earth, filling them with a presence, a life, a loveliness before unknown! Then, too, what unutterable argument is here, for mutual love, for fidelity to every holy claim, for cheerfulness and courage and hope and aspiration immortal! Then how sounds in our ears that great word, God! We know, alas! what it was to the childhood of many of us, — so dull, so gloomy, so repulsive, — but *now*, signal and security for infinite joy! Then how is that blessed being embosomed in infinite light, raying out ineffable splendors upon the universe around!

Cut off that friendly light that beams from the eternal throne; leave us nothing but bare and abstract unity and spirituality; leave us nothing but unbending fate and eternal order, and where shall our natures flee for refuge and rest? Who and where is he, that can stand in this mighty and mysterious universe, independent and alone? And who is so unobservant and stupid as not to feel that more than life itself is the spirit of life; more of every scene in which we live, is our inward impression than our outward possession? Place us in any dwelling, any palace, filled with every possible luxury and comfort, filled with beautiful works of art; and let it be the house of an enemy, of a tyrant, or of one who cares not for us, and it would be hateful to us, — its splendid apartments, its festal lights, its gems and gold, all hateful; but let it be the house of our friend, of our dearest friend, and it is pleasant to us; it is a place of freedom and rest, no matter what house it be.

It is much to believe in God. That which we believe in, so believing, is a stupendous reality. But if I may believe that God is our Father, that his is an infinitely loving nature, my whole and inmost being dissolves in joy and gladness at that truth. It is not grateful to me, I will confess it, — this demonstrative character of the pulpit, this free utterance of what is inmost and most sacred. I would rather meditate, often, than speak. But this common, this vital and all-comprehending good, which we *all* have in the knowledge of that Infinite Being, in whom we live and have our being, — this privilege of uttering the word *Father*, when we speak of God, — meet it is, for the sake of our gratitude and trust, that we should set it forth, as the chief blessing of our existence, the stay of our weakness, the resource of our affliction, the assurance that all is well;

a light above the brightness of day, a life that partakes of the infinitude of life, a joy unspeakable and full of glory.

I scarcely know how to express the need of this great reliance. It is as if I should undertake to say how much I need the air I breathe, the light to shine, or the friend that is dearer than life. A mind *may* wander away from the Parent-Mind; it may wander into the thin abstraction, the breathless void of pantheism. I will say nothing to reproach it now; my own mind might so wander; but *this* would be inevitable, — I should feel as if the fountain-life of my spirit were dried up; my strength would wither; my sun would have gone down; and cheerless and dread and mournful would be the spectacle of nature, as a human body out of which the soul had gone and left it but a beautiful idiot; my being would have lost its centre, — the centre on which hangs all life, being, blessing. *Blessing!* — the word would have no meaning; there would be no blessing on earth, no benediction in the heavens; an orphaned soul would be every reverent and true soul; seeking a Parent that it should never find, and wandering in recklessness, distraction, and despair through a boundless void. Instead of this, we have and hold the faith which Jesus teaches, of a Father in heaven.

Let us now come to the second article of the original Christian creed. "In the name of the Father" is the expression of the first. "*And of the Son*," — this is the second tenet of faith. And I have said that the place which Jesus assigns to himself in the great commission under which the new religion was sent out into the world, is the assumption on his part of more than human dignity.

Let us put aside for a moment our *faith* in this matter, and contemplate the manifestation of Jesus Christ as a mere historic fact; let us look at him as invested with attributes and claims, concerning which the most sceptical have no doubt.

For, in the position which the Christ occupies in the world, in his character, in the very ideal of him drawn in the New Testament, it is necessary to explain in some way a very wonderful thing. Jesus is not an unmeaning figure in history; it is not one that can any way be passed by. On the contrary, in the entire range of all recorded knowledge of men, from the beginning of the world to the present day, he is the most conspicuous personage; nay, he stands alone, he is taken up, out of the range of all comparison; indeed, his isolation, the unapproachable solitariness of his grandeur, as men have conceived of it, has been greater than the wise and thoughtful may have wished: but so it is. Such is the ideal; so it exists and reigns, and has reigned for many ages.

Whence did it spring? What was the original shrine of its manifestation and seat of its power? No school of Grecian intellect nor throne of Roman dominion, but a humble village-life in Judæa, — no regal court, nor learned institute, but a manger for its birthplace; obscure families and poor disciples for its companionship; a cross for ignominy, and a forgotten tomb for burial, — that is all. I do not mean to lay undue stress upon the *Hebrew* origin of this miracle of time. It would have been in fact more wonderful, if it had appeared in Greece or Rome. For the spiritualism of the Hebrew *books* was certainly the greatest in the world. But the humility of its origin shows that, for its unparalleled impression upon the world, it has been indebted, not to circumstances, but to its own inherent force and grandeur.

Now somebody drew the picture of this extraordinary being, and of his wonderful life and teaching. The record purports to come from his disciples. It has every appearance of coming from eyewitnesses; the early Christian communities received it as such; and it is not easy to doubt its genuineness. But suppose it *were* doubted; one thing at least is certain, — *there must have been an original for this picture.* Nobody could have imagined it. There is not the slightest indication in ancient literature of any ability to do this. But if you feel that no one man could do it, conceive of the utter impossibility of several writers having agreed in drawing the lineaments of such a character and life, *unless* the original had existed. And really, with reference to the moral impression upon my own mind, it is no matter who wrote the Gospels. Let it be the disciples or somebody else; or let it be, if any one pleases to say so, that it is a myth, — that the popular impressions in any way wrought themselves into the Evangelic story. Take any theory, however untenable and baseless, and it does not disturb the fact. For there, I say, stands the Great Ideal, as to all its leading traits, in unchallenged majesty and beauty. What am I to think of it? What is the rational account that I am to make of this astonishing phenomenon?

Let me suppose that I come fresh, and every way unprejudiced, to the reading of the Evangelical narratives. Let me suppose that I have never read them before, and have now fallen in with them by chance. In my study of the world's history, which I have pursued under the conviction of a providential order in it, I have come down, let us suppose, to the Christian era, and I open the Christian records. I know what has gone before. I have seen one era of progress opening upon another, and have observed that *noticeable order of things*, by which at the head of all these eras have stood great and shining men to preside over them, — Confucius, Menu, Zoroaster, Abraham, Moses, and Socrates. I know all these men; I have studied their life; I have studied their character; I have studied their words.

But how inevitably and how inexpressibly should I feel, on reading the life and teaching of Jesus, that here was a new thing in the world,—something far in advance of all that had appeared before. I am not anxious to separate this excellence from all other; I only say, that it is above all. Simply as an impartial student of history and of human nature, I say, "This is *greatest!* — this is the greatest that has ever appeared among men!" It is not *I* that say this, as a *disciple;* sceptics have agreed with believers in this testimony, and fifty generations of men, on the broadest and brightest field of human culture, with one voice have echoed the words of the Roman Governor, we "find in him no fault at all." This, I say, — taking nothing for granted, having nothing to do with critical or historical questions, — is the simple and unbiassed, and indeed irresistible, impression which every reader takes from the story of Jesus. I should be blinder than the Jewish officers sent to take him, if I did not say, "Never man spake like this man," and never man lived like this man. I should be more prejudiced than the Roman soldiers who crucified him, if I did not exclaim, "Truly this was the Son of God!" Such deep wisdom, such heart-penetrating insight into all human evil and need and sorrow, and such divine power to extricate humanity from its bondage and misery; such fearless courage and such winning tenderness united; such rebuke, and yet such pity; such plainness and such delicacy, such loftiness and gentleness, such majesty and sweetness, such love and patience, such spotless purity, such faultless perfection! — never has a being stood elsewhere upon the earth like this. And I find, too, as I read the history of subsequent times, that nearly twenty centuries, in their solemn train, have brought offerings — "myrrh and frankincense and gold," ay, and affections, tears, and worship — to the shrine of this heavenly purity and loveliness; and if I believe in any providential order of things on earth, I must believe that this place has been assigned to the mission of Jesus, by the will and appointment of Heaven.

Surely, in all this there is no extravagance. On the contrary, it all comes short. And all that men think yet, about the Christ, comes short. So wrapped about with a false and factitious drapery has been this character, that none of us have seen its full glory. The Life of Christ is yet to be written. I mean, that the true and great comment is yet to be written. We have had histories of the Christ; but, for the most part, how cold, dull, technical have they been! scarcely, indeed, readable. The Life of Jesus is yet to be written. This metaphysic discussion about the bare person of the

Christ, — Trinitarian or Unitarian discussion, — alas! how far is it from the reverent and loving contemplation of that divinest beauty! No, it is an effluence from the highest perfection; it is an outburst into this world, of a heavenly splendor; it is a pitying sorrow and sacrifice for poor and erring humanity; it is God with us; — this is the mission and glory of Jesus. And seeing this, nothing in the New Testament is hard or strange to me. *Miracles!* The *moral* miracle makes every other easy of belief. And most reasonable it seems, also, that Jesus Christ should speak, as no other being ever did, of his relation to God, of God's love and approval of him, of his reign over the coming ages, of his seat at the right hand of the Father; and when he commissioned his disciples to teach the nations, that he should command them to teach "in the name of the Father, and of *the Son*, and of the Holy Ghost."

"And of the Holy Ghost." The meaning of this third tenet of faith remains to be set forth. It is the breathing of the Spirit of God in the hearts of men. It is God, not only as above humanity and the paternal authority and goodness, or as teaching and leading it by his Son, but as *in* humanity. This is a great and momentous truth, the practical complement of all other truths. For if a divine life were not breathing *in* the soul, no power from *without* could help us. It is an everlasting truth. Many seem to conceive of the Spirit of God as if that power were introduced into the world by Christianity. But no, it is only now more distinctly recognized, as for ever in the world. From the beginning, through all ages, the Spirit of God has moved upon the moral chaos of the world. And since it *is* a chaos, since darkness and discouragement are ever brooding upon the heart of man, it is a most necessary truth. Man, it tells us, — this poor, frail man, — is not earth and dust, is not animal instinct and passion alone, is not forsaken of his Maker; there is a Spirit of God causing itself to be heard and felt in the deep recesses of his heart.

You will not understand me, of course, to speak of this Spirit, or spiritual manifestation of God, as a personality distinct from God himself. What conceivable need is there of such a distinction! We call it the Spirit of God, because it is God manifested in the spirit, — in the spirit of man; manifested as the wind that bloweth where it listeth, of which we hear the sound, see the effects, but know not whence it cometh, nor whither it goeth.

There *is* such a mysterious power abroad among men. Reckon up all the visible and known forces in the world, — the volcano, the earthquake, the storm, the lightning; bring into the account all human faculties and agencies, — reason, will, passion; and there is yet left a power not included in the estimate, — "a still, small voice," but to the spiritual nature, louder than the thunder, swifter than the lightning, deep-penetrating beyond earthquake throes. What *is* it? What is it that in spite of will, in spite of all that man can do to resist it, shakes the soul of the guilty transgressor? It is the Spirit of God. What *is* it that makes all base self-indulgence feel itself to be so mean, so poor, so low, — that will not let it hold up its head, and claim the honor and comfort of virtue? It is the Spirit of God. It is a power beyond, above, independent of man. What was it that made the bad, bold Anthony bow his head between his hands for three days, when he fled from the battle of Actium, to follow his guilty paramour of Egypt? The poor, proud, wretched Anthony did n't want to feel so; he could n't help it. And what is it that breathes the sweetness of all holy thoughts through the soul, — that flows over our darkened, humbled, prostrate humanity, like heaven's morning light over the night-bound and overshadowed earth? It is the Spirit of God.

There is a power in the world, that is not set down in any of our categories of human purposes or human wills. There is a power that holds up the human world from sinking to utter ruin; that arrests lawless license; that restores decaying civilization; that revives dying religion; that feeds the wasted fountains of holy inspiration. There is a power that awes the bad, and cheers the good, and supports the stricken, and stands by the martyr in his agony; yes, and will stand by us in the silent strife and agony of our hearts to be true and faithful. It is the Spirit of God. Strong and tender, powerful and pitying, almighty and all-merciful, — there is a spirit of God within us.

Such I understand to be the comprehensive and cardinal faith of Christianity,— faith in the Father, and the Son, and the Holy Spirit. Such, I have no doubt, was the faith of the primitive churches and ages; afterwards wrought by fanciful speculation into the hard, dry, abstract dogma of a metaphysical Trinity. Such I could wish had been our own and only profession of faith, as a Christian body; and indeed such substantially it has been, and is. For we never liked this scholastic dispute about the persons in the Trinity; and have engaged in it only because it has been forced upon us.

There was a work published a few years ago, entitled "Hippolytus and his Age." Hippolytus was Bishop of Portus, the port of Rome, at the mouth of the Tiber, late in the second century. The work consists of a book of Hippolytus on Heresies, discovered not many years since; and of sundry theses and discussions connected with it, by the Chevalier Bunsen, long the Prussian Ambassador in England, a man of eminent learning and worth, and held in high honor and confidence both at home and abroad.

Mr. Bunsen states the cardinal points of the Christian creed in the following terms:—

First, the Unity of God, as the eternal *Father*, is the fundamental doctrine of Christianity.

Secondly, the *Son* is Jesus Christ as the adequate manifestation in the highest sense; every true believer is Son, in a state of diminishing imperfection, being brother to Christ in the Spirit. But Jesus alone is the incarnation of the Word (Λόγος). He therefore is called by St. John "the only begotten" (*Unigenitus*).

Thirdly, the Spirit has not had, and is not to have, any finite individual embodiment; it appears in finite reality, only as the totality or universality of the believers, as the congregation of believing mankind called Church. But this Spirit, substantially, is not the spirit of any human individual, or of any body of men, but the Spirit of God.

"This," says Mr. Bunsen, "is the statement of the Bible; and to accept and believe this statement as the revelation of divine truth, this, and this alone, forms the doctrinal test of the Apostolical age."

Thus speaks a man of reputed learning and orthodoxy; and with his statement we entirely agree.

Is not the time coming, is it not *near*, when this mystifying, misleading, and, I am tempted to say, irreverent controversy about the scholastic dogma of the Trinity, is to give place to the simple and solemn Evangelic verity and truth "of the Father, of the Son, and of the Holy Ghost"?

This simple verity takes hold of the heart; and I must not finish this exposition of the Christian creed without distinctly saying in close, that no creed can avail us anything, unless it restores, reforms, regenerates the soul into the image of God, into the imitation of Jesus Christ, into communion with the Spirit of the All-pure, the All-holy. To be born again, — not once only, as coming into this world, but to be born again spiritually, — of the Spirit of God; to renounce our selfishness, our self-will; resolvedly, and by a true repentance, to put away every sin; to welcome, and embrace with a loving heart, God's love and mercy; to find this strength in all temptation, and this resource in all affliction; to be true and pure, to be free and fearless, to be humble and patient, to be submissive and thankful, to be gentle and to be strong; to make our life all sacredness and goodness; to make our spirit all sweetness and devotion; and thus to be happy, a thousand-fold beyond all that this world can make us, — thus to be happy, say rather *blessed*, in time and in eternity; — this, and this alone, is the consummated and inly-working faith of Christianity, — the faith of "the Father, and of the Son, and of the Holy Ghost."

THE END.